DATE DUE

The
Personal
Intelligences

Promoting

Social and

Emotional

Learning

Launa Ellison

CORWIN PRESS, INC.
A Sage Publications Company
Thousand Oaks, California

For information:

Corwin Press, Inc.
A Sage Publications Company
2455 Teller Road
Thousand Oaks, California 91320
E-mail: order@corwinpress.com

Sage Publications Ltd.
6 Bonhill Street
London EC2A 4PU
United Kingdom

Sage Publications India Pvt. Ltd.
M-32 Market
Greater Kailash I
New Delhi 110 048 India

Printed in the United States of America

Library of Congress Cataloging-in-Publication Data

Ellison, Launa, 1944-
  The personal intelligences: Promoting social and emotional learning /
by Launa Ellison.
        p. cm.
Includes bibliographical references and index.
  ISBN 0-7619-7691-4 (cloth: alk. paper)
  ISBN 0-7619-7692-2 (pbk.: alk. paper)
  1. Learning, Psychology of. 2. Learning—Social aspects. 3.
Teacher-student relationships. 4. Classroom management. I. Title.
  LB1060 .E449 2000
  370.15'23—dc21   00-008746

This book is printed on acid-free paper.

01 02 03 04 05 10 9 8 7 6 5 4 3 2 1

Corwin Editorial Assistant: Catherine Kantor
Production Editor: Denise Santoyo
Editorial Assistant: Candice Crossetti
Typesetter/Designer: Danielle Dillahunt
Indexer: Pamela Van Huss

Contents

Preface   viii

  Acknowledgments   xi

About the Author   xiii

1. In the Beginning . . .   1

  Consider the Brain   3

  The First Day   5

  The Second Day   7

  Shapers of My Thoughts   9

2. Learning and Stress   18

  How About Play?   19

  Identifying Stress   20

  Soothing Ourselves   22

  Food and Stress   25

  Choices, Rhythm, and Support   26

  Teaching Emotional Vocabulary   27

  "I" Statements   28

  Emotion Puppets—The Fulls   30

  Reading Nonverbals   32

Freeze Frame   35
Putting Skills to Use   39

3. Emotions Affect Learning   **41**
Intrapersonal More Than Emotions   42
Discrimination Meter   45
Developmental Issues   46
The Biology of Emotions   50
The High Road and Low Road   53
Reflective and Reflexive   54

4. Personal Intelligences
Across Curriculum   **57**
Symbolic Messages   57
Two-Hour Work Blocks   58
Class Record Book   59
Friendly Helpers   62
Healthy Bodies Influence Brains   63
Body Systems   65
Research Reports   66
Arts Experiences and Symbolic Messages   70
Ruby Bridges   70

5. Reflection, Goals, and Portfolios   **73**
Student Reflection   75
Knowing When You Know   76
End of the Day Reflection   78
Goal Setting   79
Andy's Goals   81
Homework   82
Halloween Scary Stories   83
Portfolios   86
Reflection and Self-Talk   89
Portfolios Again   92

6. Children in My Life   **94**
Matt—Bright and Has ADD   95

Kaelyn—Bright and Insecure   97

Tim—Bright and Sensitive   98

Tara—Struggling With Learned Helplessness   99

Jacob—In Crisis   100

Halimo—Somalian Refugee   103

Seth—"I'm Not Doing Nothing."   104

Andy—Too Many Changes   105

7. Our Diversity   **108**

Diversity of Perceptual Strengths   109

Extraversion and Introversion   110

Graphing Diversity   111

Self-Management/Impulse Control   113

Mindfulness   114

Learning Who We Are—MBTI   117

8. Nurturing Independence   **125**

Rubrics   130

Content, Collaboration, and Choice   130

Empathy   133

9. Expectations and Resources   **138**

Expectations   138

Resources   146

End Points   **158**

Resource A: Books Connecting to Personal Intelligences   **163**

Resource B: Powerful Learning   **171**

How Students Learn   172

The Schools Our Children Deserve   173

Resource C: A List of Emotional Vocabulary   **181**

References   **184**

Index   **189**

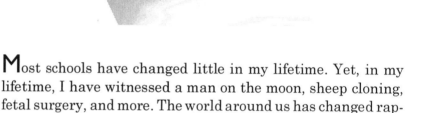

Preface

Most schools have changed little in my lifetime. Yet, in my lifetime, I have witnessed a man on the moon, sheep cloning, fetal surgery, and more. The world around us has changed rapidly and significantly.

When I was a beginning teacher, there were a number of theories of learning. Educators had little knowledge of how the "black box" brain worked. One theory stated that children were empty vessels waiting to be filled. Another theory promoted B. F. Skinner's concept of operant conditioning, the forerunner of behavioral management systems. These theories are significantly different from our present understanding of how learning occurs.

Fifteen years ago, most evidence of brain functioning was deduced from observing damaged brains. An injury in a specific spot of the brain was documented and the resulting dysfunctions were noted. Today, scientists learn about brain functions with new technology. Images of the brain are recorded with computer-facilitated Positron Emission Tomography (PET scans), Magnetic Resonance Imaging (MRI), functional MRI, and Single Photon Emission Computerized Tomography (SPECT), as well as electroencephalographs (EEGs).

These research techniques have contributed to the new understanding of the strong interplay between emotions and thoughts. Research also confirms the importance of the frontal cortex for reflective processing. The frontal cortex continues to develop into our 30s.

Changes in technology have stimulated outer space adventures, challenged traditional business practices, and affected even what we eat. Educators' new understandings of the brain must now influence their educational practices. Teachers understanding this book will be able to link brain research to intrapersonal and interpersonal intelligence. These personal intelligences, including our emotions, are the core of how we manage our lives. Personal intelligence includes the thousands of decisions relating to our body-brain system—how we care for our bodies, how we react to life's experiences, how we deal with stressors, and how we deal with others.

The first three chapters of this book will help educators understand the role of brain stem and midbrain functions, which relate to classroom environment. A safe, caring community is not simply a "nice" thing; it is a prerequisite for our brains' optimal functioning. The lifelong skills of identifying our stressors and soothing ourselves can, and must, be taught in our classrooms. Noticing and naming emotions, our own and others, are lifelong skills. The first three chapters of this book link the biology of emotions to important developmental issues of children.

Chapter Four identifies symbolic messages communicated by what we choose to do, or not do, in our classrooms. One message may be that we are not comfortable with our own emotions. Another message may communicate that we believe, or do not believe, children can make effective choices to manage their time and be independent learners. This chapter encourages teachers to think about the symbolic messages within their curriculum in the context of developing personal intelligences.

Chapter Five focuses on student reflection. The frontal cortex is responsible for reflective thinking, evaluating, setting goals, and monitoring plans. The chapter explains ways to weave reflective thinking into weekly classroom experiences.

Chapter Six, with fifth- and sixth-grade students as examples, illustrates the diversity of issues and needs within our classrooms. In Chapter Seven, issues of diversity and personal intelligence are explored in more detail. Diversity is broader than racial identity. There is a vast range of diversity in our perceptual strengths, our self-management skills, and our levels of mindfulness. Teachers and students profit from understanding the diversity of their personality types and preferences, as well as the diversity of intelligences.

In Chapter Eight, two fifth graders are compared as an indepth example of diversity. One child is an independent learner and the other is struggling. One has secure habits of inner self-talk, the other does not. Differentiated instruction is clearly needed to foster the success of these two children.

The last chapter focuses on expectations and resources. All school districts have goals or expectations for curricular areas. My district has specific health curriculum expectations that link to self-management. The business community strongly states its expectations that reflect the personal intelligences. The New Haven, Connecticut, schools have led the way, by teaching components of the personal intelligences at every grade level. This chapter provides links to helpful resources.

Does neuroscience tell me exactly what to do in my classroom? No. Does recent neuroscience research provide ideas for improving education? Yes, in three areas relating to Intrapersonal and Interpersonal Intelligences. First, emotions drive attention. Because a child can learn little without focusing attention, teachers must deal with each child's emotions for effective education. Second, our human brains seek to make meaning out of experiences. Meaning is a personal construction. Teachers must link to what a child already knows, feels, and understands in order to facilitate meaningful connections. Third, no one functions well when under stress; thus helping children learn how to identify and cope with stressors is an important educational issue. Educators become more effective as they understand the basic premises of brain functions.

> The task, then, is for educators to deeply understand the way in which the brain learns. The more profound the understanding, the easier it is to actually see what is happening in a classroom and to creatively introduce the necessary changes.
> —Renate Nummela Caine and Geoffrey Caine, *Making Connections: Teaching and the Human Brain,* p. 174

The personal intelligences are foundational skills. They are the skills of self-management. Children who have the skills of personal intelligence learn traditional academics more efficiently.

This book connects recent understandings of neuroscience with classroom practice. It provides a depth of information on brain functions. It encourages educators to focus on developing lifelong skills related to personal intelligence. This book is written for classroom teachers, though it will be helpful for parents, principals, and graduate classes.

In this book, I share my classroom practices linking brain functions with the development of Intrapersonal and Interpersonal Intelligence. I affirm what Gardner (1999b) writes in *Intelligence Reframed:* "I want my children to understand the world, but not just because the world is fascinating and the human mind is curious. I want them to understand it so that they will be positioned to make it a better place. . . An important part of that understanding is knowing who we are and what we can do" (p. 181).

ACKNOWLEDGMENTS

"Influencers are unlikely to achieve success unless their story is genuine, one that grows naturally out of their own experiences and touches the lived experience of their audience."

Howard Gardner, *Extraordinary Minds*, p. 118.

This quote has been posted on my refrigerator throughout the process of writing this book. Repeatedly, teachers comment that my first book, *Seeing With Magic Glasses,* touched their lives. They could feel themselves watching as the story of my classroom unfolded. This book is a second glimpse into my classroom, my children, and my teaching practices. I am writing of my own experiences, not a recipe for you to recreate. Each of us needs to sift the wisdom of our mentors with the spice and style of our own lives. Teaching is a creative, exciting endeavor, with each day uncovering new ingredients.

During the winter of 1996, Bob Sylwester gently twisted my arm over dinner, "When are you writing your next book?

You have more to say." As I drove him back to the airport the next afternoon, after his presentation, he nudged once again, "Have you thought about your next book?" "Yes," I replied. "It is about the importance of developing Intrapersonal and Interpersonal Intelligences."

To my mentors—Bob Sylwester, Howard Gardner, Marian Diamond, Candace Pert, and Eric Jensen—I give admiration for leading the way.

I want to thank the Minneapolis Public School District and the corresponding AFT selection committee for granting me a half-year sabbatical to begin work on this book.

I give thanks to Sandi Bandli, my sabbatical substitute. She graciously allowed me full access to "my kids" so I could write early each morning and still interact with the children. I found I needed to teach in order to "hear the children's voices" and be able to write with greater clarity. A daily dose of real children kept my focus. Sandi gave me the opportunity for partnership as I wrote. I thank student teachers Terrylee Trevola and Angie Grace, who shared experiences with me along the way.

A special thanks goes to my mother, Arlene Swanson, for her nurturing support and helpful suggestions throughout the process of writing this book.

In addition to the individuals mentioned above, the contributions of the following reviewers are also gratefully acknowledged:

Robert Sylwester, Emeritus Professor of Education
University of Oregon, Eugene, Oregon

Kathryn McNaughton, Faculty of Education
University of Regina, Regina, SK Canada

Gogi Dickenson, Professor
University of Texas at San Antonio, San Antonio, Texas

Jolinda Simes, District Mentor Teacher
Edina, Minnesota

I dedicate this book to all of the children from whom I learn and to you, the readers, who share my passion to help each child reach his or her full human potential through a firm foundation of Intrapersonal and Interpersonal Intelligence.

About the Author

Launa Ellison currently teaches fifth and sixth graders in the Minneapolis Public Schools, and began teaching in 1964. She has taught children in first grade through eighth grade. She is the author of more than 20 professional journal articles. Since 1984, she has published "The Consortium for Whole Brain Learning," an international newsletter dedicated to improving educational practices through understanding brain research. She has trained teachers in Singapore, South Africa, Bangladesh, and Canada. Her first book about brain research and her classroom practices, *Seeing With Magic Glasses,* is used as an undergraduate college of education textbook.

In the Beginning . . .

It is the end of August, and my thoughts turn to my school-room. This year greets me with special challenges. My school is a mess. My classroom space is in a different location, and the security of known neighbors has changed. Each one of these changes is enough to shake the comfort of children.

For many years, children and parents had been invited to our school the week before classes begin. They are invited to a "Meet Your Teacher" teatime. It is a simple event that calms and reassures the spirits of both child and parent. This year, this invitation is not possible due to construction, and thus I expect the first day of school will be unusually unsettling. Parents, anxious that their children be valued and nurtured, will escort their children to my classroom. Children, anxious that they find friends, will tentatively enter the room. Children, parents, and teachers come with unsettling thoughts, unspoken fears. Yet this is a good place to begin this story about how I strive to develop the personal intelligences of my students. It is a story of emotions and a story of educational priorities.

Our emotions are the core of our humanness. Calm emotions release the brain's attention to the processes we call "thinking." We are awash in our emotions. Thus, our focus begins with emotions.

My school has been under construction for a year. We have coped with jackhammers, construction dust, huge trucks, and piles of materials and equipment. The construction should have been finished by now. It isn't. We are short three classrooms. The concrete sidewalks to our doors are still in process. Our halls are stacked with construction materials not yet used and educational materials hoping to be used. The school office is not completed, and office equipment is not in place. Our usual "Welcome to the new school year" letters from the teachers to the children cannot be sent because the computer system storing the children's addresses has no place to function. Both the teatime and the letters were, in previous years, designed to facilitate a smooth start. In the past, these traditions fostered the productive rhythm of our first school day.

It will be good when the construction is over. Our school has never had an assembly room in which we all could fit. The construction process will give us this space. Our school is on a half city block, and we have lived for many years with outbuildings, prefab isolated classrooms plopped on a slab of concrete in our playground. The outbuildings dwarfed what little space we had for children to play. Eventually, when the construction process is finished, our children will have space to play soccer and basketball. But for now, we must focus on safely getting the children through the unfinished messes and into the building. Just seeing the mess is disconcerting.

Emotions. My emotions. Parents' emotions. Children's emotions. Life overflows with emotions. Foremost in my mind is creating a classroom environment that calms and stabilizes our collective emotions.

Due to the reorganization necessitated by the construction, my classroom location has changed. The new room's door is in a different spot, not nicely set in the middle of the wall as I was used to. Thus, using my same furniture, I need to create a new environment.

Behind my new door is a jumble of stacked furniture. A tangle of tables and bookcases is edged with a mound of boxes. My task is to create a large common space for our whole-class meetings and smaller spaces for students to work and gather in small groups. My student teacher and I begin. The couch is positioned as the cornerstone of our meeting area. Shelving for the hundreds of paperbacks, our class library, is nestled next to the couch. The area is defined by a table and cabinet. A nook is created for a soft chair and two floor pillows. A circle space is formed for a reading group. Tables connect to room dividers, providing students with smaller, more secure spaces and a bit of privacy.

As our classroom slowly begins to take shape, it begins to feel like we can live here. When materials are unpacked from boxes and plants green the room, all of us will feel the benefits of a thoughtful room design. This room design is a far cry from the traditional layout, where teachers' and students' desks line a room, enclosing territories. Our classroom space is shared space. Shared community space gives a subtle but very different message than having assigned student desks as individual territories. By using this room design, I state my intention that we will grow together as one community. Students will learn how to be a community and how to live respectfully with others' needs and desires. We learn respect by living with respect and by experiencing respect. This room will respect all of the children.

My priorities, as I begin this year with this group of 25 children, reflect my understanding of the brain. First, I must help each child feel emotionally safe in our classroom and in our school. The traditional voice inside my head states, "School is about learning, about doing the work, not about emotions." I counter with the words of David Hubel, co-recipient of the 1981 Nobel Prize in Medicine, "If you understand the brain, you understand learning, and if you understand learning, you understand education." Many of our educational practices in the past have not been based on an understanding of the brain.

CONSIDER THE BRAIN

Our brains have three levels of processing: the brain stem, the midbrain, and the cerebral cortex (the convoluted outer layer of our brains). In the 1970s, Paul MacLean, a scientist working in the Neurophysiology Laboratory at the National Institute of Mental Health, labeled these levels the *Triune Brain*. The first level, the brain stem, is a couple of thickened inches where the spinal cord becomes the brain. MacLean's system labeled this region the *Reptilian* brain because reptiles have these basic brain functions. The brain stem continually monitors our body processes: Is there enough water in the system? Is the heartbeat correct? How is the blood pressure? The brain stem monitors our breath, our nervous system, our digestion, our hormones—the whole works. The brain stem includes the Recticular Activating System (RAS), from a Latin word meaning *small net*. The RAS monitors every body system to check if it is in balance. If not, it alerts the body to make the necessary corrective adjustments. This balance, known as homeostasis, is critical for our survival. It is fully developed at birth. The brain stem receives sensory information from all over the body at a rate of 100 million messages each second; thus, the RAS must discard unimportant information. The RAS is a selective system. It saves only that which needs attention, that which is unusual, that which is out of the ordinary. The brain stem continuously asks, "Shall I pay attention to this? Is this important? If it is important, where shall I send the information?" Attention is first focused on the body. The first level of my students' brain processing is focused on the physical environment of the classroom. "This room is too hot." "This chair is too short." "I'm hungry and thirsty." "School starts too early, I'm not awake." "Where is the bathroom, and when can I go?" "How long do I have to sit here?" The RAS directs our conscious attention first to the comfort and maintenance of our bodies.

I begin the school year as I begin each day, aware of the need to calm the brain stem system. My classroom environment must be normal and safe. Yet, to engage the brain stem in its constant search for discrepant events, something new must happen—a new science object, a new display of artifacts.

The brain stem also monitors for stress and relaxation. Stress creates body responses preparing for escape. I do not want stress in my classroom. I want students' bodies to be calm so they can effectively tap into higher levels of brain processing. Thus, in these first days I teach relaxation skills. This tiny brain stem area, two inches, is the first processing level in our brains.

The second level of brain processing is deep inside our brains in a region called the midbrain. MacLean's term for this area was the *Limbic system* or the *Old Mammalian* brain. The word *limbic* comes from the Latin word *limbus* meaning "border." Early researchers believed this area was the border between the brain stem and the real brain, the neocortex. The thalamus, hypothalamus, hippocampus, amygdala, and pituitary are part of this region. This region processes emotions and memories. Recent research, however, has revealed that emotional processing is not limited to this region. Emotions are processed in many areas of our bodies. Just as the RAS is continuously processing sensory information from the body, the structures in the midbrain continuously process our emotions. We are never without emotions, but like the RAS, most of the processing never reaches the surface of our consciousness. Unimportant messages are thrown out, like junk mail, before they are opened.

> Brain science is a burgeoning new field, and we have learned more about the brain in the past 5 years than in the past 100 years. Nearly 90 percent of all the neuroscientists who have ever lived are alive today.
> —Pat Wolfe and Ron Brandt (1998), "What Do We Know From Brain Research?" *Educational Leadership*, p. 8

THE FIRST DAY

As my students come through the door on the first day of school, I am consciously aware of these first two levels of brain processing. I must deal with the brain stem and the midbrain to effectively get to my students' cerebral cortex, the new cortex of convoluted gray matter most people think of as the brain.

My goals for the first days of school are to:

- Create community
- Establish a sense of trust
- Nurture friendships
- Establish respectful behavior
- Establish normal routines
- Begin to deeply know my students— their interests, their styles, their skills, their concerns

I teach children. The children are my focus. This is a very different attitude from, "I teach math." My focus makes a world of difference. My intent is to help children learn. To facilitate students' maximum learning, I focus on their whole brain, and that means paying attention

> The emotional system tells us whether a thing is important—whether we ought to put any energy into it. We've basically ignored emotion for years. We didn't know how to regulate it, to evaluate it, or to measure it. We've told kids that school is for learning and memorizing, and if they want to have emotion, have it at recess or after school. Or, if we're going to have emotion in school, we'll put it in art class. The biggest single problem of our profession is that we never learned how to deal with emotion in school.
> —Robert Sylwester, "The Brains Behind the Brain," *Educational Leadership*, p. 25

A community of learners reflects a classroom ethos different from that found in traditional classrooms. In the traditional classroom, students are perceived as relatively passive learners who receive wisdom from teachers, textbooks, or other media. In the community of learners classroom, students are encouraged to engage in self-reflective learning and critical inquiry. They act as researchers who are responsible, to some extent, for defining their own knowledge and expertise. In the community of learners classroom, teachers are expected to serve as active role models of learning and as responsive guides to student discovery processes. Teachers learn to provide instruction on a need-to-know basis, which allows them to respond to students' needs, rather than a fixed scope and sequence schedule or an inflexible lesson plan.
   —Ann Brown and Joseph Campione, in *How Students Learn*, Nadine Lambert and Barbara McCombs (1998), p. 153

to their safety concerns, their fears, their friendships, and their emotions.

On the first day, after the children leave, my student teacher and I reflect. What did we learn that will guide our thinking about these individuals? We learned that many of these children like to read. Many children focused intensely on books during our 45-minute silent DEAR (Drop Everything And Read) time. In hushed conversations we asked each child what he or she had read recently and what books were their favorites. Many children quickly described their summer adventures with books. These children read orally with good expression.

We also learned that some children do not like to read. They had difficulty focusing. Some had great trouble finding a suitable book out of the hundreds on our bookshelves. Some chose books that were too difficult. When asked to read, they stumbled, faltering as they attempted to make sense out of the print.

Asked what they read over the summer, their shoulders shrugged. Within these few minutes, I knew these children were not comfortable with reading. These are the children I need to understand better.

One of our first tasks in a classroom community is to know each other. "We're going to start spelling right away. This week you will learn each other's names and how to spell them. I'll give you a list of everyone's first names. Does anyone want a shortened version of their name?" Niko responds and so does Kate. We will continue to review students' names throughout the week. On Friday, we will test. I will point to a child, asking her to stand, and the rest of the children will write her name. This simple activity does two things. First, it creates an incentive for students to identify the child and name. Second, it gives me a feel for the children's ability to memorize spelling words. It becomes obvious which children need help in phonetic strategies.

This afternoon, we paired students to learn two strategy games, Othello and Nine Man Morris. Homemade game boards allowed the pairs to all play at once. These games establish a common experience for all our children and are available for "in between" moments. Watching the games, we learn more about these children's personalities. Some children connected comfortably with a partner, whether or not that person was previously known. Other children essentially hid behind the structure of the game, barely communicating. Each moment is an opportunity for me to observe children's behaviors and make mental notes on individual needs. To facilitate the greatest learning in each child, I must know that child. I must know each child to plan for that child.

> *When we understand that building caring classroom relationships is the key to creating a successful learning community, we naturally design the first weeks of school to help everyone feel comfortable and learn about each other—and we integrate these opportunities into our academic programs and into the life of the classroom throughout the year.*
> —Joan Dalton and Marilyn Watson (1997), *Among Friends*, p. 10

THE SECOND DAY

On Tuesday we begin to have a sense of routine: a circle meeting for news and sharing, a specialist class, art for two weeks, then music, and so on. This is followed by a teaching meeting lasting about 20 to 30 minutes. A two-hour work time takes most of our morning—children choose what to do and in what sequence.

Then there is the children's lunch, in the room. Teachers have lunch while the children are at recess.

Journal/Reflection time is next with soft, calming background music. Another teaching meeting is followed by activities in science or social studies cooperative groups.

Finally, we settle down for 45 minutes of quiet reading. We end our day together by recording our reading and discussing the end-of-the-day reflection. It is a full day!

> *Knowing my students and my subject depends heavily on self-knowledge. When I do not know myself, I cannot know who my students are. I will see them through a glass darkly, in the shadows of my unexamined life—and when I cannot see them clearly, I cannot teach them well.*
> —Parker Palmer (1998), *The Courage to Teach*, p. 2

We chose to have our students eat lunch in our classrooms. It is a time of friendship building. This second day, just before lunch, we discuss the lunch routine. I ask, "Do you think it would be polite, if you were at a restaurant having lunch with friends, to get up and leave as soon as you were done?" In some communities this question may not work because it may not connect to some children's experiences. In my school, the question is appropriate. "No," children reply. "You have to wait until everyone is done." "That's respectful," I affirm. "So when you're in a group eating here, please wait for everyone to be done before you clean up." This simple practice stretches children's awareness of others as well as encourages cooperation with others. In a few weeks, we will introduce the idea of "inviting" friends from other classrooms to eat in our room. Right now, we need to establish guidelines in our own room.

At our teachers' lunchtime on the second day of working with these fifth and sixth graders, we reflect on how much we now know about our children. The children had completed their first drawing/writing assignment relating to our year-long school theme, "Many Doors, One Roof." The assignment was simply to draw a door and write about what's on the other side. The drawings ranged from purposeful detail to haphazard scribbles. One child used lined paper—turned the opposite way—apparently oblivious to the purpose of the lines. Another child used capital letters randomly throughout her sentences and no punctuation. One girl's sentences were elegant as she developed her intricate story. Some children's imaginations were calm and portrayed a sense of gentle beauty. A few children portrayed doors opening to violence. Other children had drawn and written so nondescriptively that their work communicated little. Regardless of the level of excellence, we posted every child's work on our bulletin boards. I purposefully begin the school year with empty bulletin boards. I want to fill them immediately with our students' work. Seeing their work in the classroom gives students the message, "I belong here." That message is very important in these first days. Second, children usually reflect on their own work in relation to others' work, thus the beginning of reflection and goal setting.

This afternoon's meeting is spent discussing the children's goals for this year and their expectations. I am listening and recording on large chart paper. Finally, I feel there has been enough exploration of ideas so that I can be directive: "So, to accomplish these goals, how do you think students (and teachers) should behave in our room?" We generate an excellent list of expected behaviors. Next week, I will ask the children to represent one of the behaviors in a large tempera painting, including a speaking bubble as used with cartoon characters.

In two days, our understanding of these children had blossomed. It blossomed because I purposefully organized experiences that would illuminate the uniqueness of my students. To teach these children, I must know these children. I explained to my student teacher, "It's beyond me how a teacher can teach a group of children in the same way. Their diversity is so evident in these first writing papers. It would even be impossible to have all of these children learn the same spelling words." To help each child grow, I must begin where that child is, where that particular child has strengths.

A Sufi story makes the point: Hodja wanted to learn to play the lute so he contacted a master teacher and asked, "How much do you charge for private lessons?"

The teacher replied, "Three silver pieces for the first month, then one silver piece a month."

Hodja exclaimed, "Oh, that's very fair. I'll start with the second month."

Too often, we try to start with the second month. The starting point must be at the beginning. I must begin with the child, not the curriculum. I must learn the child. Already I have learned a lot about these children's reading and writing, but the core of the child is not his level of math or her ease in reading or writing. The core of the child is who she believes she is and how she interacts with others. This core is represented by the Intrapersonal and Interpersonal Intelligences as defined by Howard Gardner.

SHAPERS OF MY THOUGHTS

Howard Gardner wrote *Frames of Mind* in the early 1980s to engage colleagues in a professional dialogue. Gardner (1983) writes, "I sought to undermine the common notion of intelligence as a general capacity or potential which every human being possesses to a greater or lesser extent. At the time, I also questioned the assumption that intelligence, however defined, can be measured by standardized verbal instruments, such as short-answer, paper-and-pencil tests" (p. ix). Gardner used eight criteria or "signs" of intelligence. His definition was more expansive than the traditional—"the way I define intelligence— that is, as the ability to solve problems, or to fashion products, that are valued in one or more cultural or community settings" (p. 7). In Gardner's recent book, *Intelligence Reframed* (1999b), he enlarges that definition to "intelligence as a biopsycho- logical potential to process information that can be activated in a cultural setting to solve problems or create products that are of value in a culture" (pp. 33-34).

Gardner uses eight specific criteria that qualify behavior domains as intelligence. The intelligences are linguistic, musi- cal, logical-mathematical, spatial, bodily-kinesthetic, intra- personal, interpersonal, and naturalist. Gardner (1993) wrote,

> I propose two forms of personal intelligence—not well un- derstood, elusive to study, but immensely important. Interpersonal intelligence is the ability to understand other people: what motivates them, how they work, how to work cooperatively with them. Intrapersonal intelligence, a seventh kind of intelligence, is a cor- relative ability, turned inward. It is a capacity to form an accurate, veridical model of oneself and to be able to use that model to cooperate effec- tively in life. (p. 9)

In the initial discussion of intrapersonal intelligence, I also stressed its origins in a person's emotional life and its strong alliance with affective factors. I continue to view emotional life as a key ingredient of intrapersonal intelligence, but now I stress the vital role of intrapersonal intelligence in a person's life- course decisions.
—Howard Gardner (1999b), Intelligence Reframed, p. 43

I believe the core of who we are and how we function is grounded in Intrapersonal and Interpersonal Intelligences. When children have a strong foundation of per- sonal skills, they manage themselves and cooperate with others. Children with well-developed personal skills can learn easily. Teachers continually affect the child's intrapersonal and interpersonal development whether or not they mean to.

What I do in my classroom, how I orchestrate experiences for children, affects each child's personal intelligence. Thus, I have grown to reevaluate my teaching practices. I under- stand that curriculum is not separate from context. When I thoughtfully create the classroom context to develop the children's personal intelligences, my students do a better job learning the curriculum. The curriculum and the context. The person and the experience. The child and human development of personal intelligences.

What, I ask, are the skills these children will need as adults? Information about the world will change as technology continues to reshape our world. Science will expound new insights. What can I provide that will be of lasting value to children? It is the personal intelligences that envelop the skills children will need in a changing world. My classroom practices reflect new understandings from brain research and the developing understanding of personal intelligences.

Educators have developed a range of linguistic, mathematical, artistic, and kinesthetic (athletic- and dance-related) programs specifically designed for various at risk groups. In addition, something that educators do is to further the development of meaningful relationships with their students. Virtually all learning happens within the context of human relationships. So, even if we do not consciously intend to influence our students in this manner, the contacts we have with individual students affect how they feel about themselves and what they are learning. Relationships do not just happen. They are facilitated by what we do. How we structure a classroom, for example, or the extent to which we reach out to students importantly determines the kind of relationship that will ensue: close or distant; caring or cold; primarily focused on academics; or attuned to other factors in addition to academic functioning.
—Jonathan Cohen (1999), *Educating Minds and Hearts*, p. 17

Who I am as a teacher and who I am as a person are intertwined. I have had important guides who facilitated my professional growth. John Dewey set the stage 100 years ago with his philosophy honoring the whole child. Dewey's Laboratory School linked curriculum with children's experiences. It recognized that we are always teaching values because all of life's experiences are value-laden. He sought not simply "to modify the traditional 'three Rs' curriculum. It is a question of the right organization and balance of our entire educational system" (Tanner, 1997, p. 37). I seek a balance and organization that is different from the traditional three Rs. The balance I seek honors the whole child. My goals include growth in traditional skills, but I purposefully organize my classroom to nurture a child's independence, her perseverance, and her self-confidence. These parts of intrapersonal intelligence are foundations for success.

Personal effectiveness is the foundation of interpersonal effectiveness.
—Stephen Covey (1991), *Principle-Centered Leadership*, p. 60

People with particularly strong intrapersonal intelligence are prized in the business world because they can make optimal use of their talents, especially under rapidly changing conditions, and they know best how to mesh their talents with those of their coworkers.
—Howard Gardner (1999b),
Intelligence Reframed, p. 200

John Dewey's school organization fostered the spirit of the child, modeled concern, and taught children how to "work out problems." Dewey's school strove to develop children's lifelong habits of accepting responsibility and cooperating with others. It had an emphasis on creative activities that produced objects of value for oneself. In the laboratory school, "adults and children really talked with one another. This point is crucial for today's schools because it has become increasingly clear that mechanical instruction—even by humans—does not feed the human spirit" (Dewey, 1990, p. 37). Too often, children and adolescents report that adults talk *at* them, but not *with* them. Talk time in my classroom is purposely designed to talk with children rather than at them.

Yesterday our classroom became a bit too noisy. A number of children had chosen to play Magic, a new card game. My student teacher felt strongly that the game was the cause of the noise and that some children were ignoring their work. She suggested we eliminate the troublesome game. I agreed that the game was the source but chose to model talking with children instead of controlling them. I began the class meeting, "I noticed this morning a lot of you were playing Magic. What are the good things about the game?" We generated a list on the chalkboard. I concluded, "Yes, you are learning things by playing Magic. What are the problems we are having with Magic?" The list of problems took form next to the original list on the chalkboard: sometimes it gets loud; watchers make comments that interfere; some people are playing when they have other things to accomplish; we're taking up a lot of space in the room. The children knew what the problems were. I didn't need to control the situation. I needed to talk with the children and help them think through the issues. "How shall we solve the problems?" I asked. A number of ideas were presented by different children. In the end, we all agreed to limit the playing of Magic to Fridays, when they are completely finished with their weekly work. They agreed to play in a certain area of our space, and there would be no watchers. This discussion modeled listening to children. It allowed students to form their own points of view and present their ideas. I guided. I did not impose. The result dealt with the issues of the game, but more important, it was a rich opportunity for students' personal development.

Sylvia Ashton-Warner (1963) was a second guide in my developing sense of what is important in teaching. I bought her book, *Teacher,* a few years after I began teaching. The cost in 1966 was apparently $1.95. That's quite a value considering I continue to re-read it! The preface explains that Ashton-Warner believes "she has discovered a method of teaching that can make the human being naturally and spontaneously peaceable" (p. 11). Ashton-Warner worked with the Maori children in New Zealand. Her work represents the true meaning of education, *educere* in Latin, meaning *to draw out* the children.

> The noticeable thing in New Zealand society is the body of people with their inner resources atrophied. Seldom have they had to reach inward to grasp the thing that they wanted. Everything, from material requirements to ideas, is available ready-made. From mechanical gadgets in the shops to sensation in the films they can buy almost anything they fancy. They can buy life itself from film and radio—canned life.
> —Sylvia Ashton-Warner (1963), *Teacher,* p. 97

Ashton-Warner's methods were a forerunner of the concept that children "construct" their minds through experiences. She wrote of key vocabulary and organic writing. She wrote of listening between the lines of children's conversation. These were powerful new ideas to me in the 1960s. I had been taught to teach at a large university, but I had not been taught to connect to children's lives. Ashton-Warner (1963) wrote,

Ten o'clock is backache time. By then you have spent an half hour bending over the children writing at their low desks. But there's no alternative. Not only do you enter the words they ask for at the back of their books, but bearing in mind the reading of them afterwards, you watch the spacing of the words for better legibility, carefully oversee the grammar and, above all, nurture the continuity of their thought. You correct as they go along, not after. It's no good sitting at the table and letting the children queue up. You've got to be mobile and available to all. You've got to exercise something like an all-seeing eye all the time and all at once. (p. 55)

In the margin next to this, I wrote, "Roam!" Apparently back in the early days of my teaching career, in the middle 1960s, I

What are the causes of the nervous exhaustion so common among teachers? This exhaustion is peculiar to American teachers, and seems to be the natural result of the general nervousness of the American people. Not only are our teachers peculiarly liable to nervous irritability, but the same mental constitution in the children causes them to be far more restless, and hence disorderly, in school than are children in most European countries. Teaching is in itself not exhausting. To those having a natural aptitude for it, it is a most delightful and healthful occupation. American teachers are worn out not by teaching, but by governing, their pupils.
—M. L. Holbrook (1884), *Hygiene of the Brain,* pp. 112-113

hadn't figured out that I needed to constantly roam. Now the idea of standing in front of the room or sitting at a desk is absolutely foreign to me. I continually roam.

At the time I read Ashton-Warner, I was not happy being a teacher. There were too many control issues in my classroom. I was teaching to the whole group and expecting, somehow, that it would work because that is the way I'd been taught. It was frustrating. As I read *Teacher,* a glimmer of light began to dawn, a glimmer of joy. There was another way to teach. There was a way to teach where I could personally know children and attune activities to a child's skills, needs, and interests. Ashton-Warner connected to the hearts of individual children and made a difference. It could be done. If she could do it, I could figure out how to do it. I went into teaching to make a difference, but I didn't have an idea how to do so.

By the mid-1980s, my style of teaching children had been changing for some time. Through a Minnesota Department of Education grant written by innovative parents, I had a new opportunity to learn. The three-year grant enabled my school to investigate "whole-brain" education. Dr. Roger Sperry had won the Nobel Prize for his "split-brain" research, which provided new insights on hemispheric specialties. Dr. Robert McKim, at Stanford University, had been producing materials to use with his engineering students on visual imagery and visual thinking. There was a renewed interest in the legacy of Maria Montessori and a better understanding of the role of our perceptual modalities—auditory, visual, and tactile (touch) kinesthetic (whole body)—as learning strengths. At St. John's University in New York, Rita and Kenneth Dunn were doing research on a learning styles model. Our educational community had begun to appreciate the vast variation of our human brains.

Who is the self that teaches?
—Parker Palmer (1998), *The Courage to Teach,* p. 7

About that time, I picked up a copy of Howard Gardner's *Frames of Mind.* I plowed through the text, which seemed to be written in Harvardese. It was not a text for teachers; it had been written for the audience of cognitive psychologists to extend the discussion of "what counts as human intellect." *Frames of Mind* marked my next level of growth. Gardner provided the framework to identify and value the wide and wonderful range of "smarts" I had observed in children.

Gardner's model of Multiple Intelligences valued our bodies, our emotions, our whole brain. Language and math were valued, but the multiple intelligence model also valued the arts—visual thinking, music, dance, and movement. Gardner, for the first time, defined personal intelligences—Intrapersonal Intelligence, the development of internal aspects of "one's own feeling life," and Interpersonal Intelligence, "the ability to notice and make distinctions among other individuals." For me, the personal intelligences represented the missing piece. I knew it was important for children to have skills in language and math. I knew that the arts communicate the essence of our cultures and speak to our hearts. The missing piece of human intelligence was valuing our internal lives and valuing how we interact with other lives. Gardner's definition of intrapersonal intelligence gave validity to my efforts to help children recognize and engage their emotions. The definition of interpersonal intelligence gave credence to my observation that people can know a lot, yet be thwarted because their people skills are troubled waters. Yes, I teach math and reading, but as I teach, I also affect the two critical arenas of Intrapersonal and Interpersonal Intelligence. With Gardner's concept of personal intelligences I found the words, the systematic schema, to purposely plan for these intelligent behaviors.

If schools are to be responsive to the needs of the whole child, then the social and emotional needs of children will have

> Intellect, emotion, and spirit depend on one another for wholeness. They are interwoven in the human self and in education at its best. By intellectual I mean the way we think about teaching and learning—the form and content of our concepts of how people know and learn, of the nature of our students and our subjects. By emotional I mean the way we and our students feel as we teach and learn—feelings that can either enlarge or diminish the exchange between us. By spiritual I mean the diverse ways we answer the heart's longing to be connected with the largeness of life— longing that animates love and work, especially the work called teaching.
> —Parker Palmer (1998), *The Courage to Teach,* p. 4

to be a more integrated and central focus of classroom teachers and school communities. Of central importance is the understanding that social and emotional factors are central parts of learning—that stability, motivation, and even attention are essentially social and emotional components of the individual. Without a stable, motivated, and attentive learner, every teacher knows that instruction is futile. So learning itself is at risk if schools fail to understand the social and emotional development of children.

Parker Palmer (1998) writes, "We teach who we are" (p. 1). My inner life still searches for a better understanding of my emotions and my relationships. Joseph Chilton Pearce writes, "What we are teaches the child far more than what we say, so we must be what we want our children to become" (Childre, 1996, p. 11). My personal search fuels my desire to help children learn intrapersonal and interpersonal skills. "Teaching holds a mirror to the soul," writes Palmer. "Good teaching requires self-knowledge; it is a secret hidden in plain sight" (pp. 2, 3). Stephen Covey affirms, "We are teaching one thing or another all of the time, because we are constantly radiating what we are" (Covey, 1992, p. 126).

The search for one's self is a valid undertaking for all of us, whether or not we teach. Gardner's identification of the personal intelligences gave validity to my personal search and guides to my purpose with children. My actions, whether I know it or not, touch the spirit of my students. We are whole, not compartmentalized. The way I set up the physical arrangement of furniture in my classroom gives messages of trust and community. The specific lessons I choose, over a variety of lessons with similar purpose, address my goals to develop children's personal intelligences in the process of teaching the curriculum. The way I use cooperative groups speaks to my expectations of student interaction. Listening to children communicates my respect for them. The myriad of decisions I make in my classroom reflects the mirror of my soul. I cannot give what I do not have. My success with students depends on my own personal intelligence.

Teachers possess the power to create conditions that can help students learn a great deal—or keep them from learning much at all. Teaching is the intentional act of creating those conditions, and good teaching requires that we understand the inner sources of both the intent and the act.
—Parker Palmer (1998), The Courage to Teach, p. 6

And so the path of my development runs through the insights of John Dewey, the life of Sylvia Ashton-Warner, and the Multiple Intelligence framework of Howard Gardner. Each of these people has been my mentor. By writing this book, I have the opportunity to give back, to mentor other teachers who choose to follow this pathway. My path is a commitment to the whole child, the whole person. We are an integrated mind, body and spirit, one whole, always affected by every part. Recent research on human emotions has led me to better understand the interwoven fabric of mind, body, and spirit in our lives. As I learn, I weave my understandings into the tapestry of the children's lives in my care.

A Sufi story describes a language teacher exclaiming, "I have a marvelous system for teaching a new language. I taught it to a man who enrolled as a private pupil. I taught him absolutely perfectly."

Asked then, "So he knows the language very well now, does he?"

"Not a word," said the language teacher. "I taught him perfectly, but *he* just *would not learn.*"

2

Learning and Stress

In the beginning of each school year, I teach my students to breathe deeply and relax. I ask them to pay attention to the stress in their bodies and to identify when they feel tense. Why? Stress, quite literally, throws one's body out of balance. Stress can stem from a number of sources—our interactions with other people, expectations we have for ourselves, lack of the nutrition our bodies desire, or undesirable chemicals in our bodies.

Robert Sapolsky (1994), writing in *Why Zebras Don't Get Ulcers,* explains the chemistry of stress. Our bodies, like zebras' bodies, are programmed to respond to life-threatening experiences. Multiple changes happen instantaneously when you are "struggling to save your neck." Breathing, blood pressure and heart rate all increase to speed needed glucose, fats, proteins, and oxygen to your muscles. Digestion and immune systems are slowed; they are long-term processes that are not important when you are "running for your life." Our senses and memory become sharper and our sense of pain is dulled. Adrenaline and epinephrine are secreted by our adrenal glands above our kidneys. A hormone, vasopressin, blocks the process of our kidneys; that process can wait until later. Our pancreas releases another hormone, glucagon, which raises the level of sugar glucose in our bloodstream for quick

Trying to operate your body without understanding its design is like flying blind.
—Barbara Levine (1991), *Your Body Believes Every Word You Say,* p. 124

18

energy. Our body is poised for the emergency. These processes are common to all mammals—you, me, and the zebra. They represent the work of the sympathetic nervous system, turned on by the four F's—fright, fight, flight, and sex. Zebras' emergency sympathetic nervous system only activates during the four F's. Humans are very different from zebras in one important aspect. Our sympathetic system can be alerted into action by our thoughts, not just by our external experiences. Our thoughts can also calm us, stimulating the other half of the autonomic system, the parasympathetic system. This calming system promotes our growth, fosters our immune system, and organizes energy storage for our future needs.

HOW ABOUT PLAY?

Many children today have significant stress. Each year, there is an increase in the amount of schoolwork children are expected to master. Children have less and less time to just play. Their time is organized around schedules for parkboard sports, music lessons, and more. Play should be imaginative and spontaneous, not organized. Neighborhoods today are less cohesive and may be more dangerous. Fewer and fewer children are allowed to simply go outside and play on their block, as I did when growing up. Parents are spending less time with their children discussing the day's events and enjoying family time. There are more families with both parents working or only one parent actively involved with the children. Instead of unstructured play, children are engaged with computer games or watching TV. There are more children on antidepressants and on mind calming drugs. There are more overweight children with few physical activities.

Informal play helps children gain social skills and learn to handle aggression appropriately. The more an animal—or a child—plays, the better its chance of becoming a well-adjusted member of

Play and spontaneous physical activity have other important functions in early life, including stimulation of the cerebellum, which coordinates motor activity, balance, and higher cognitive functions. In early childhood the child is naturally impelled to jump, hop, spin, and interact with playmates. (Organized sports do not qualify as "play" in the same sense because they are structured by adults and lack spontaneity.) Because the cerebellum is integral to many mental skills, restricting physical play may have serious long-term consequences.
—Jane Healy (1998), *Failure to Connect*, p. 224

the society. "Through play bouts, an animal's aggressive tendencies are socialized and brought under control," states Dr. Stephen J. Suomi of the National Institute of Child Health and Human Development. "Play seems to make the difference in quality of life, between merely surviving and really thriving."

The level of a child's play correlates with intelligence, language development, general well-being, and the ability to understand others. Play reduces stress. It also enhances late creativity and original thinking. As children use symbolic objects to "pretend," they are broadening mental landscapes and building abstract abilities. It is very troubling to hear from preschool teachers that stimulus-saturated young children are losing the ability to play spontaneously.

IDENTIFYING STRESS

Yet, who is teaching our children how to manage their stress? We, teachers, must—for effective learning. Teaching children about stress must be part of our routine curriculum in classrooms simply because children learn better when they are calm. Children's emotions can promote learning, or their emotions can inhibit learning. Teaching children to recognize when they are stressed is the first step toward managing stress.

I ask students to reflect and write a response to "How do you know when you are stressed?" Children's responses vary.

"I don't know when I'm stressed."

"I feel frustrated."

Optimal health requires accurate information about what you feel and need.
—Barbara Levine, Your Body Believes Every Word You Say, p. 124

"I get butterflies in my stomach."

"I get a headache."

"My brain is all confused, and I can't think."

I explain to my students that our bodies give us information. We need to listen to our bodies and know when we feel stressed. When we are able to identify that we are stressed, we can then use some strategies, like breathing, to release our stress.

Mike explains, "When I'm home and I get stressed, I take a hot bath."

Stacey shares, "When I'm stressed, I don't talk. I won't say anything."

In the process of our discussion a child creates a distur-
bance. I get stressed. My voice tone changes. When the incident
is over I say, "I just got stressed. Did you know I was stressed?"

"Oh yes," the children respond.

"How did you know I was stressed?" I ask.

Numerous children respond:

"Your voice got higher."
"Your face got red."
"You looked hard."

I comment on how some of the children look when they get
stressed. "Mike, when you get stressed you get an uncomfortable smile, and some people think you aren't taking the situation seriously. Kyle, when you get stressed your face gets
tense." I encourage students to notice nonverbals to tell if another person is tense. This discussion begins, but only begins,
to help students be aware of their response to such situations
and their reactions to stress. I will continue to revisit this idea
many times throughout the year.

Handling our emotions is a learned skill that affects the
rest of our lives. It is an ever-present task. One of the essential
emotional skills is learning to "soothe ourselves," by taking a
positive action to calm oneself. Some adults have difficulty
soothing themselves. They come home frustrated, and reach
for a beer or a glass of wine. They sit in front of the TV, smolder-
ing. Some parents may end up yelling at their children, when
their real frustration was activated hours ago and they haven't
soothed themselves.

Daniel Goleman used the phrase "emotional hijacking." He writes,
"the hijacking occurs in an instant, triggering this reaction crucial
moments before the neocrotex, the thinking brain, has had a chance
to glimpse fully what is happening, let alone decide if it is a good
idea" (Goleman, 1998, p. 14).

Researcher Joseph LeDoux refers to the two ways of emotional
processing as the low road, an automatic reaction, and the high
road, which includes the frontal lobe processing (LeDoux, 1996).

Educator Robert Sylwester uses the terms *reflexive,* an immediate
response, and *reflective,* a response after we've considered
alternatives (Sylwester, 2000).

SOOTHING OURSELVES

Too many children do not have adult models who soothe themselves appropriately. Recent research on the brains of infants and toddlers find that when adults don't know how to soothe themselves, their children don't learn to soothe themselves—and the cycle goes on. Children learn by copying others. Calm adults are needed in children's lives, if not at home, then through programs like Big Brothers/Sisters. Actions always speak louder than words. Children learn more from watching how adults behave than from listening to what they say.

Stress is part of life. Rather than trying to shield children from all stress, we'd do better to make sure our children's stresses are "child size." That way, they can begin practicing stress-management strategies (and at an early age) instead of becoming overwhelmed.
—Georgia Witkin (1999), *KidStress*, p. 198

I ask my students what they do to calm down when they are angry or disappointed. Children know the "right answers," and respond with such ideas as making a positive plan of action, exercising, listening to calming music, deep breathing, playing with their pets, going for a walk in a park, and connecting with plants and animals. Still, these skills have not been internalized, and the children who are most reflexive do not calm themselves well enough to take appropriate action to handle their emotions positively.

For many children our schools play a major role in teaching them how to handle their emotions. It is not a question of whether or not we want our schools to take on this responsibility. We *must* take the responsibility. Children learn from the models around them. Children who see emotional hijacking at home are the same children who react reflexively at school. All children need practice in handling their emotions, because it is a developmental issue, but children without positive home models are especially needy. These same children have little self-awareness of their emotions, they are often the least mindful, and they are the least able to focus their attention. It is a developmental troublesome threesome.

What factors contribute to not being in touch with our stress? In our own childhood we may have experienced different scenarios. As a small child you get a small hurt, "Ow!" Mommy or Daddy rushes to you and puts a Band-Aid on the hurt. The unspoken message is that you need outside help with a problem. A better strategy might have been for Mommy or Daddy to comfort you and ask you, "How does it feel? What do you think you could do to make it better?" The internalized message is different.

The prefrontal cortex is the brain region responsible for working memory. But circuits from the limbic brain to the prefrontal lobes mean that the signals of strong emotion— anxiety, anger, and the like—can create neural static, sabotaging the ability of the prefrontal lobe to maintain working memory. That is why we say we "just can't think straight"—and why continual emotional distress can create deficits in a child's intellectual abilities, crippling the capacity to learn.
—Daniel Goleman (1998), Emotional Intelligence, p. 27

An opposite scenario plays out like this: "That can't hurt. Be a big boy. Big boys don't cry." In other words, don't listen to your body's feelings. The message is "just cope, and don't cause a problem." Unfortunately, you learn to discount the messages from your body. Yet messages from our bodies contain significant meaning. Our brains are designed to scan the vast stimuli we are exposed to and give us feedback on discrepant events, events that need some attention. If we are not encouraged to develop a sensitivity to our bodies' messages, we lose important feedback. We lose touch with our bodies and our responsive emotional tenor.

I ask my students, "What is the only thing you will have all of your life?" They ponder the riddle. "Your body. Your body is the only thing you have from birth to death. It is very important that you learn how to take care of your body." And once again we breath deeply, all the way to our stomachs, to calm and balance our bodies. When we relax, the natural cells that guide our immune systems increase. We promote our own health.

A new sixth grader, with very poor behavior, recently wrote me a note stating he was getting sick because of the stress in his life. I was pleased he made the connection. He's made the first step. My task is to help this overweight, irascible boy understand that his internal habits are the cause of his discomfort. He has the habit of "awfulizing" with an overgeneralized "the whole world is against me" attitude.

Stress actively disassembles the system—tissues are shrunk, cells are destroyed.
—Robert Sapolsky (1994), Why Zebras Don't Get Ulcers, p. 140

Teachers often complain that we are stressed. We are stressed by meetings, by wanting more time to prepare, and by trying to control students' behaviors. Controlling consumes energy. I prefer to teach my students to be responsible for their

Breathing Tips to Teach Relaxation

Position your thumb on your belly button. Notice that your fingers cover your stomach a few inches below your navel. Focus your attention on that area of your stomach. Breathe in slowly focusing on filling that lower stomach area. Your stomach should bulge out. Continue to breathe in, letting the air begin to fill your rib section. Finally, fill your chest, letting it expand outward. Hold. Start to exhale by gently contracting your lower stomach area and slowly moving up. Each of the three steps should take about 6 seconds. Breathe in 1. . . 2. . . 3. . . 4. . . 5. . . 6. . . Hold 1. . . 2. . . 3. . . 4. . . 5. . . 6. . . Breathe out 1. . . 2. . . 3. . . 4. . . 5. . . 6. . . After I teach children the rhythm of six, I eliminate the count and use the words, "Breathe in, relax. Breathe out, smile." We repeat the process until the children are calm.

There can be many variations of breathing for relaxation. One we especially like is "Ahh." When you exhale quietly make an "Ahh" sound. Another nice exhaling sound is "ou" as in the word "soup." Another variation is exhaling in twelve or more short spurts. You can ask the children to imagine a color that makes them feel calm (or happy, or focused) and breath in that color. You can do one-sided breathing by holding your right nostril shut and breathing, in that same slow way, with your left nostril. This process stimulates the opposite side of your brain. Left-nostril breathing registers in the right hemisphere. Be sure to balance by doing both nostrils.

Teaching Muscle Relaxation

Another relaxation method is learning to tense and release muscles. This can be done sitting or standing. I start with our hands and move to all parts of our bodies. "Boys and girls, today we are going to learn another way to relax. We'll start with your fingers. Hold your hands in front of you and stretch, stretch your fingers. Stretch them, stretch them, stretch them, relax. Now stretch your arms. Stretch them up, up, up. Stretch them over your head to the left. Now over your head to the right. Stretch. Feel your arms pull your sides. Relax. Now focus on your shoulders. Stretch them out and back. Stretch. Now stretch them up. Stretch. Stretch. Relax. Focus on your chest and stomach. Stretch. Stretch. Stretch. Relax. Now focus on your legs all the way down to your toes. Stretch. Stretch. Stretch your whole leg, your toes. Relax. Relax every part of your body. Relax."

You can do the same sequence using the words, "Tighten, tighten, tighten, and relax." I prefer stretching because when children tighten their hands they make a fist. The imagery of a fist, to me, blocks the relaxation process.

—Adapted from James Humphrey (1988), *Teaching Children to Relax,* and Philip Smith (1980), *Total Breathing.*

own behaviors. I model the behaviors I want from my students. I've had to learn how to identify my own stressors and learn relaxation strategies. It sounds so obvious—"You can't teach something you don't know." We are more likely to get sick when we are stressed because our emotions change our immune functions. When we, as teachers, learn relaxation strategies we are able to teach our students to relax. After students have really internalized relaxation, I am able to use it to help refocus energy in our classroom.

> An important factor in a person's resiliency was whether he had developed an "internalized" locus of control— the perception that he is the master of his destiny—or an "externalized" locus—in which he tends to perceive himself as having little control over the events of everyday life.
> —Robert Sapolsky (1994), *Why Zebras Don't Get Ulcers,* p. 256

Identifying stress, and learning how to reshape your responses with breathing or exercise, is important. A critical factor in dealing with stress is the belief that you have choices, that you're not stuck with the problem with no way of solving it. When you believe you can affect the outcome, that you have some control over the situation, there is less stress. Stress is increased when the situation is unpredictable and you feel you have no support system to help you.

If I were an executive in a health maintenance organization, I would be lobbying to mandate that children be taught to listen to their bodies in order to be aware of stress. I would lobby that schools teach children deep breathing and relaxation techniques so the techniques become ingrained habits. In the long run, the costs of health care would be significantly reduced by stress/relaxation habits.

FOOD AND STRESS

What we think about a situation can cause stress in our bodies. What we put into our bodies affects our stress level as well. Our children are eating more and more processed foods and ingesting more food additives. I ponder the long-term results of stress caused by processed foods and additives.

> The evidence suggests that amino acids in the food we eat can have profound effects on depression and anxiety as well as our concentration, motivation and memory.
> —Blair Justice (1987), *Who Gets Sick: Thinking and Health,* p. 108

Short term, it is clear that foods affect our moods. Brain chemistry is changed by the supply of nutrients available from recently eaten foods. Foods high in carbohydrates, like many snack foods, increase the brain's level of serotonin, which results in a calming effect. A high-carbohydrate breakfast or lunch can be too calming and lower children's alertness. Sweets release endorphins, which are natural opiates; thus, by eating them we medicate ourselves. Proteins are crucial for good brain functioning. Marian Diamond reports on an eight-year study of 2,000 Guatemalan children taking protein supplements. The researchers found the children "grew and developed skills faster, had more energy, and made better social and emotional progress than children the same ages who consumed less protein" (Diamond & Hopson, 1998, p. 85). What we put into our bodies obviously has an effect on our body-mind system. Unfortunately, our schools' federally regulated breakfast program has little protein and is high in carbohydrates. It seems to me it's time for recent brain research to affect practical decisions, such as what is a healthy breakfast for our low-income children.

Stress also is connected to a sense of helplessness. If we think we can't do anything about our uncomfortable situation, the anxiety turns to stress. I meet far too many children who have learned to be helpless. Somehow they have decided they aren't in charge of their lives, that they are not responsible for their own learning. They feel life is being done *to* them, that their actions won't change anything. They live continually with a low-grade stress of helplessness.

It is very clear that stress inhibits good attention and learning. I strive to help my students recognize when they are stressed and help them learn strategies to relieve their stress.

CHOICES, RHYTHM, AND SUPPORT

These caveats on stress translate into choices, rhythm, and support in my classroom. My students have many choices. They have the choice of where to sit. They have the choice of which assignment to do first and which to do later. They have the choice of working hard in class and having no homework, or focusing on an art project, discovering more microscopic animals in pond water, playing chess, and having the potential of more homework.

Our class time has a predictable daily rhythm. Children learn that our life together has a normal flow. On Monday, children create their individualized spelling lists. Wednesday, they work in a cooperative group to practice their spelling, and on Friday, the partners test each other in a round-robin fashion. Tuesday afternoons, we are "Friendly Helpers" for first and second graders, part of our school's extensive cross-age pairing of classes. Friday afternoon, if their work is done, individuals have choice time, which includes games and additional arts and crafts. There is a rhythm to our days, a rhythm that guides the predictability of our week together.

There is also support. At the beginning of the school year, I repeat, over and over, "I want to help you. If you are confused about something, don't waste your time staying confused, ask for help. Ask me for help or ask a friend for help. Just don't stay confused. Smart people ask questions. Asking questions is very important. I want your brain to be turned on, not stressed because you don't know something. Therefore, ask questions!"

TEACHING EMOTIONAL VOCABULARY

When we have words for an idea we are better able to distinguish the embedded subtleties. The Inuit people have more than 25 words for the subtle differences of snow. The average temperature in Bangladesh varies only 25 degrees Fahrenheit throughout the year, yet the people recognize six different seasons. In Minnesota the average temperature varies 120 degrees, from—20 to 100—yet we claim only four seasons. Emotions are our biological thermostat, constantly registering dangers and opportunities. Knowing vocabulary that describes emotional differences enriches our sensitivity to the nuances of life.

Most children come into my room with an emotional vocabulary equivalent to "mad," "sad," and "glad." Early in the year, I work to enlarge their vocabulary and thus their sensitivity to the emotional hues of their experiences. As in most classrooms it only takes a few days for one child to have irritated another. This is my opportunity to introduce the children to "I" statements to expand their repertoire of words.

"I" STATEMENTS

"This year, boys and girls, we are going to use 'I' statements when we are frustrated with someone else's behavior. An 'I' statement begins with 'I am _____ (a feeling word) when you _____ (the specific action that just happened) and I'd like you to _____ (the behavior desired).' The other person responds first by acknowledging what the person felt and identified: 'I understand you are _____ (the exact same word the first person used) when I _____ (the exact description the person used) and you'd like me to _____ (the exact behavior described by the first person).' The second person can then give his own 'I' statement, reversing the roles. When students learn to really listen to one another's feelings, they often learn to respect that person." As I talk, I post the process on the board. This word pattern will take its permanent place on the wall above the chalkboard, visible from all angles in my classroom.

I role-play the process with an imaginary problem, then ask my students what problems they have encountered in other classes. After we've generated numerous problem ideas, I ask students to practice the process in partners. There is a buzz of activity. Within minutes I ask for volunteers to demonstrate for the class what they have just practiced. Jim and Mike share their role play about taking a pencil. Lee and Kaelyn share the "I" statements about sitting too close to someone. I explain, "This process is powerful because it starts with 'I' and listens to the information your body is giving you. Your body registers emotions before you have words for how you feel."

I give Niko a gentle shove and whisper for him to shove me back, then ask, "What if I shove him back again?"

The children have all seen similar situations and they respond, almost in unison, "He'll shove you back and it will keep going."

Antonio Damasio (1999) writes in *The Feeling of What Happens:*

> The pervasiveness of emotion in our development and subsequently in our everyday experience connects virtually every object or situation in our experience, by virtue of conditioning, to the fundamental values of homeostatic regulation: reward and punishment; pleasure or pain; approach or withdrawal; personal advantage or disadvantage; and, inevitably, good (in the sense of survival) or evil (in the sense of death). Whether we like it or not, this is the *natural* human condition. But when consciousness is available, feelings have their maximum impact, and individuals are also able to reflect and to plan. They have a means to control the pervasive tyranny of emotion: it is called reason. Ironically, of course, the engines of reason still require emotion, which means that the controlling power of reason is often modest. (p. 58)
>
> In a typical emotion, then, certain regions of the brain, which are part of a largely preset neural system related to emotions, send commands to other regions of the brain and to most everywhere in the body proper. The commands are sent via two routes. One route is the bloodstream, where the commands are sent in the form of chemical molecules that act on receptors in the cells which constitute body tissues. The other route consists of neuron pathways and the commands along this route take the form of electrochemical signals that act on other neurons or on muscular fibers or on organs (such as the adrenal gland) which in turn can release chemicals of their own into the bloodstream. (p. 67)
>
> Having feelings is of extraordinary value in the orchestration of survival. Emotions are useful in themselves, but the process of feeling begins to alert the organism to the problem that emotion has begun to solve. The simple process of feeling begins to give the organism *incentive* to heed the results of emoting (suffering begins with feelings, although it is enhanced by knowing, and the same can be said for joy). The availability of feeling is also the stepping stone for the next development—*the feeling of knowing that we have feelings.* (p. 284)

"Will the problem escalate or settle down?"

"Escalate. It will get to be a big trouble."

"When have you experienced a little problem turning into a big problem?" Students share their stories. I end the discussion by saying, "I'm going to expect you to use 'I' statements to solve your problems when they are little. If you need help while you learn how to do this, please let me know. The purpose of an 'I' statement is to solve the problem by talking to one another, instead of getting frustrated and getting physical."

The next day, I have a real opportunity to use the process with two children. One starts, "I feel . . ." The other child, glancing at the posted script to quickly refresh his memory, returns the statement. The process is simple, efficient, and effective. The two children hear one another, the tension is gone, and we all return to the matter of learning academics.

When we are emotionally uptight, energy stays in a negative emotion. None of us, including children, focus well when emotionally distracted. Our brains are wired to alert us and keep the emotional issue in our attention until that particular "threat" is solved. There is no sense to continue teaching, because the child won't learn until the child can release the negative emotion. Thus, I do my best to help children solve problems as quickly as I can. In the long run it is more effective to stop and solve the problem. I do not feel this is an imposition. In fact, these bits of assisted intervention may be the most important part of my day with a child. I certainly don't expect fifth graders to enter my class knowing fifth-grade math, so why would I expect them to know fifth-grade interpersonal problem-solving skills? As I teach the child to identify her feelings, put them into words, learn a strategy for dealing with the other person involved, and resolve the difficulty, I am teaching life-long strategies. I am forming tomorrow's citizen.

EMOTION PUPPETS—THE FULLS

A few days later I begin the process of enlarging students' repertoire of emotional words. I begin, "What words do you know that mean the same as 'glad'?" We generate a list using a purple marker. Students offer "happy," "excited," "joyful." I enlarge the list a bit with words like "appreciated," "victorious,"

Panta writes about the Fulls: One day Peacefull was walking down the sidewalk looking for someone to play with. Peacefull saw Stressfull doing his work. Peacefull walked over to Stressfull and asked, "Can you play with me at the park?"

"No, I can't play with you," Stressfull said angrily.

So, Peacefull went somewhere else to find a friend to play with.

When Peacefull left, Stressfull was alone. It didn't feel good. Then Stressfull went to find Peacefull, to see where she went.

Finally Stressfull found Peacefull asking Powerfull to play. When Stressfull got to Peacefull, Stressfull said, "I'm sorry, but I am lonely now. Will you play with me?"

Peacefull said, "Sure, I'll play with you." Then Peacefull, Stressfull, and Powerfull played together until 7 p.m.   The End

"elated," discussing the subtleties of each. Then, very dramatically, out of a cloth bag that has been hidden close by, I reveal "Powerfull," a felt stuffed doll. It is purple with gold stars.

Regally, I move around the group introducing Powerfull to the children. Then I reposition myself next to the list of "glad" words. "What is Powerfull feeling appreciated for?" I ask. My students give a number of responses. I continue, "What is Powerfull feeling elated about?" The discussion continues. Finally we decide where Powerfull will reside in our classroom. The children choose to have it be on the top of the bookshelf in our circle area. "Powerfull may sit with you during our workday. Powerfull needs to be returned to that place whenever we leave the room, for recess, and at the end of the day. If more than one person wants to have Powerfull, which is usually the case, please use 'I' statements and make a deal about how long each of you will have Powerfull."

For the rest of the week I intersperse powerfully positive feeling words into our conversations, both with the whole class and with individual children. Our awareness of the sense of power and the students' sense of the subtleties significantly expands during this week.

In the next weeks I present Peacefull, turquoise with a silver heart, and Joyfull, yellow with a great smile. I choose to focus on these three positive emotions first. Each time, I use a matching color of construction paper to record words the children already know and the words I introduce to expand their vocabularies.

We have focused on these positive puppets for three weeks. It is close to Halloween when I decide to bring out Fearfull. We discuss our fears and make lists of words that link to being fearful. This process of investigating an emotion is fairly familiar now. I introduce Numbfull, a new concept. Numbfull is a larger gray doll who has a stomach pocket. The creator, Barbara Kobe,[1] explains, "Numbfull is gray for a purpose. When we stuff our feelings or try to hide them, we lose our color. We look and feel like a gray cloudy day. Numbfull's message is that when feelings are unexpressed, they have a stifling immobilizing effect on our bodies, our faces, our minds and spirits."

I stuff Fearfull into Numbfull's stomach pocket and ask, "Have you ever stuffed a feeling?" Oh yes, they explain. And once again stories abound.

During the next weeks, I repeat the process of introducing a new stuffed character. Tearfull represents sadness. Blue Tearfull befriends us when we feel tearful. Red Ragefull represents our anger. He helps us figure out what to do when we are angry without hurting himself or others.

The process of using the Fulls has taken eight weeks, two months. My children have had time to process significant emotions. Boys and girls have enjoyed the company of stuffed companions. All of us have enriched our vocabularies; many have used these emotion words as part of their spelling lists. The Fulls are now a part of our classroom community.

For many weeks emotion words fill our consciousness, developing the children's vocabulary and their understandings of the subtleties of emotional words. In the process, my students have become better able to identify and reflect on the emotional qualities of their own lives. We have all grown.

READING NONVERBALS

The following week I continue this lesson by listing two columns on the chalkboard: Positive Emotions / Negative Emotions. I place Powerfull under the positive column and Stressfull under the negative. I use my "Emotions Vocabulary" flash cards,[2] which portray emotions using drawings of eyes, noses, and lips. I show the line drawing of "optimistic" and ask the children to point to the column the expression belongs to. They point to positive. I show "hostile" and then "frightened." Children quickly point to negative for both words. We continue with "interested," "thoughtful," "angry," and "hopeful." Each time the children point to the correct classification and I place the drawings, one by one, on the chalkboard tray. On some of these depictions, the lips, the smile, is not that distinct. I ask, "How can you tell these feelings apart?"

"The eyes," some children respond.

"The eyebrows," others chime in.

I squint my eyebrows in a frowning question and ask, "What do the eyes do?"

"Like you're doing now!" Michelle squeals.

"Everybody, make your faces like mine." The children are quick to make frowning faces. I ask, "How does that make you feel, in your stomach and all over your body?" Children respond with words like "tension," "stressed."

I continue, "Figuring out how someone feels by noticing their body and face is called reading their nonverbals. What does the word *nonverbal* mean?"

Sam provides a beautiful explanation about how it's not words but it has meaning. I continue, "Raise your hand if you can tell if a teacher is in a bad mood." Hands shoot up, eager to share their insights. We discuss their experiences for a while, then I stand with my hands on my hips, in a stiff pose, and use a sweet voice modeling, "Boys and girls, today we will . . ." Then, without finishing the sentence, I ask "Am I in a good mood?"

"No way," they respond.

"Why? How do you know? My words were fine."

"Your body wasn't OK," one child returns.

"You were all stiff."

"It felt icky," another ventured forth.

We discuss how the body and face can express one emotion and the words express a different emotion. "What information does the body and face give you compared to the words?" The children easily verbalize that our bodies tell what we really feel. We can use words that are opposite to what our bodies are saying.

"Can you remember a time your body and your voice gave opposite messages?" Again, the children share their stories.

New research provides convincing evidence that violent criminals have poorly functioning brains. Low verbal IQs, attentional problems, impulsivity, poor school performance, inadequate processing of information, inflexibility, restlessness, agitation, and difficulty processing social cues are all characteristics commonly associated with criminal behavior.
—Robin Karr-Morse and Meredith Wiley (1997), *Ghosts From the Nursery*, p. 54

Most children tacitly know how to read nonverbals. I am just confirming what these children know. I am bringing clarity to the unspoken truths they have processed since they first responded to their mother's smile or lack thereof. From infancy our brains have been taking in emotional signals and making decisions on how to react. Very early we learn, nonverbally, that we won't get the love we want from a face drawn with depression or tight with anger. We know this deeply. Reading nonverbals is essential to our emotional danger-warning sys-

---

A summary of Oliver Sacks' (1986) chapter on nonverbal knowing, "The President's Speech" from *The Man Who Mistook His Wife for a Hat*, p. 76:

"What was going on? A roar of laughter from the aphasia ward, just as the President's speech was coming on, and they had all been so eager to hear the President speaking. . . ."

"There he was, the old Charmer, the Actor, with his practiced rhetoric, his histrionics, his emotional appeal—and all the patients were convulsed with laughter. Well, not all: some looked bewildered, some looked outraged, one or two looked apprehensive, but most looked amused."

Patients in an aphasia ward have lost the ability to understand words. Why then were they laughing? Although they were not understanding the words, these aphasiac patients were understanding the nonverbals, the not words, of the president's message. Clear messages were being communicated by his posture, gestures, facial expression, as well as the intonation of his voice.

On the other hand, Emily D., a former English teacher with agnosia, had essentially the opposite condition. She listened, stony-faced, for Emily D. could no longer tell if a voice was cheerful or angry. She processed only the words, not the intonations of meaning. Emily D.'s reaction was clear: "He is not cogent. He does not speak good prose. His word-use is improper. Either he is brain-damaged, or he has something to conceal."

tem. Some children, however, have experienced so many disparate messages that they are not at all sure what the confusion of emotional signals means. These children often miss critical clues. Bullies often misread nonverbals. Research indicates that incarcerated prisoners also show a lack of skill in reading nonverbals.

Our discussion of nonverbals can begin to help children understand. This discussion brings nonverbals out of a tacit, unspoken realm, and into our open shared knowledge in our classroom. I will be able to refer to noticing nonverbals as we process experiences throughout the school year.

I continue our discussion by showing some of the more subtle expressions. We compare "bored" and "hopeful," then "embarrassed" and "lonely." I show the "alienated" picture and ask what the feeling represents. Niko responds with the word "small."

"Yes," I affirm. "When I feel alienated I do feel small!" I am expanding the emotional vocabulary of my students, which enables them to understand the nuances and hues of our life experiences.

FREEZE FRAME

I continue to the next part of this lesson, the Freeze Frame process created by the Institute of HeartMath. I pass out papers divided in three sections. The first is labeled, "What is the stress?" As I hold Stressfull, I ask the children to draw pictures of a situation that they remember as really stressful. I continue to softly give ideas of possible stressful situations as students begin drawing with their colored pencils: "Maybe something happened on the playground or on the bus that was stressful. Maybe you have gotten angry at someone at home and that was stressful. Maybe . . ."

I become quiet and give them time to draw. I notice one boy has already finished his undetailed picture. I know this boy is depressed. One of his goals is to be more in touch with his emotions. I simply observe. Another child has a handful of colored pencils and is choosing to use only yellow. I can hardly make out his drawing. I know his life is unsettled, moving weekly between his mom and his newly remarried father. I am pleas-

Stress is an untransformed opportunity for self-empowerment and self-security—a challenge rather than a threat.

—Doc Lew Childre (1995), *A Parenting Manual*, p. 31

antly surprised with other children's clear articulation of a stressful scene. I wait, encouraging individual children, until it feels time to share. Many children willingly share their picture images of recent stressors. Others are reluctant to share, their stressors still too raw.

I ask, "How does your body feel right now after drawing your picture?" Children share upsetting body feelings.

"I feel nervous."

"My stomach is tight."

I draw a simple representation of the brain on the chalkboard. "Stephanie, I notice you get stressed out when you are hungry. Right? Your brain shuts down. You lose your concentration and you get grumpy." She nods. "Your brain can't think right because your body needs food." I draw in the area of the brain stem at the top of the spinal cord, the two inches at the base of the brain. "Stephanie, your energy is getting stuck. You can't get to the higher thinking levels of your brain to learn your math because this bottom part of your brain is taking the energy, saying, 'Body is hungry, body is hungry,' so you need to learn to bring a snack or tell an adult what you need. You need to learn to understand your stress and solve it, so you can concentrate." Stephanie nods, acknowledging her feelings. "Stephanie, would you talk to your mother and try to bring snacks from home? If you don't have a snack and you need food to concentrate, please ask me for a granola bar. OK?"

"Tim, you were really frustrated with Sam and Mike hassling you at recess. You couldn't start working after recess. Your emotions were stuck here." I draw in the area of the midbrain. "When you are emotionally upset, your thinking stays stuck and you can't focus on 'learning'—whatever the lesson is."

Stresses can lead to what Daniel Goleman (1998) labels "emotional hijacking." As the children drew their stress pictures, they recalled the stress and their bodies reacted to the stress. We humans can cause ourselves stress and create a stress reaction just by thinking about a stressful situation. We can also learn skills to release that stress and get into our heart intelligence in order to change our physiology. Being in a better mind/body state allows us to create better solutions to our problems.

Doc Childre, founder of the not-for-profit Institute of HeartMath, defines HeartMath as "the psychological equations of heart intelligence." His system is designed to "help people achieve continuity in mental and emotional balance and more effectively access their own intelligence" (Childre, 1995, p. 11). Childre writes,

> In the past decade, scientists have discovered that repeated stressful reactions, such as frustration and anger, cause nervous system imbalances which are detrimental not only to the physical heart, but upsetting experience can reduce the heart's pumping efficiency by 5-7%. Other research at IHM (Institute of HeartMath) has shown that remembering upsetting experiences also depletes the immune system for many hours. IHM researchers found that just one, five-minute episode of mentally and emotionally recalling an experience of anger and frustration caused a depletion in Immunogloulin A (IgA) for the next six hours. (p. 23)

I continue, "It's important that we learn to deal with our stress so we can go on with our lives. Look at the middle section of your paper. In that section draw a place or a situation where you feel really good, where you feel these positive emotions on our list. Draw what gets you into your heart."

The simple activity I'm leading my students through now is a result of pondering how we can help children learn to integrate their brain intelligence with their emotional, or heart, intelligence.

The children draw the wonderful safe places in their lives. They draw friends and family. They draw a special place in their yard or park. They draw running and other exercise. Children intuitively know what makes them feel calm and happy. They have been learning these important life lessons since babyhood. Unfortunately, only rarely have children been encouraged to make this self-knowledge explicit. Rarely have children been encouraged to think about these issues in order to learn to use their innate understanding to guide their lives.

I ask the children to notice how their bodies feel now. "Show me with your fingers, on a scale of 1 to 5. Does your body feel

Figure 2.1. Freeze Frame

SOURCE: Institute of HeartMath. The FreezeFrame Picture design was excerpted with permission from *Teaching Children to Love.* © Planetary Publications (1996).

different now that you've focused your attention on something that makes you feel safe and happy?" Hands indicate that the children are clearly in touch with the changed state of their bodies. We go on to discuss their body sense and share pictures. A child describes being at her grandma's house. Another child tells how he feels when he's playing with his dog. There is a felt shift of energy.

In the third section of the paper, I ask the children to think about their original stress, but not to lose the good feelings in their hearts. "With that good feeling in your heart, draw a solution to the original stress you pictured." Ideas seem to pop into the children's imaginations because they quickly picture solutions. The group's energy remains calm. This part of the discussion is easy. Students have great ideas for solving their stressors. I ask, "When your heart was calm, was it easier to solve your problem?"

"Yes, yes, yes," I hear echoed around the room.

"Then, when we have a real problem, let's practice going to our hearts before we try to solve it." We wind up this discussion, and I hope for opportunities to help students practice "going to their hearts."

PUTTING SKILLS TO USE

Allen comes in from recess huffing and puffing. He is really angry! Apparently Jerod tickled him under both arms repeatedly, even when told to stop. Allen is intent on "pounding him." Jerod is nervously trying to start his work, but his body language tells me he is very aware of Allen. Allen is loud and moving rapidly. I ask Allen to find his heart space and breathe. I tell him we'll deal with his frustration with Jerod when he is calm in his heart. I walk away and deal with other children. In minutes I return to Allen. He says he's ready to talk, but his body language doesn't look calm. I explain his body language looks as if he needs more time to get into his heart, and leave him again. When I come back a second time Allen looks better. I ask if he's ready to give "I" statements to Jerod. He is. I get Jerod. Jerod has calmed some but is still quite apprehensive.

Allen begins, "I feel . . . (violated, I suggest) yeah, I feel violated," he starts to smile, "when you try to tickle me under my

Conflict resolution, however, is not a purely cognitive enterprise or a rational weighing of options. It involves other capacities as well: the ability to empathize and a moral sensibility, both which stem from mastery of the different levels of emotional development. Successful conflict resolution requires the ability to put yourself in another's shoes, to acknowledge and empathetically experience the other's objectives.
—Stanley Greenspan (1997), *The Growth of the Mind*, p. 234

arms." The smile is broad now and Jerod starts to smile also. "And I want you to stop," Allen finishes with almost a giggle.

Jerod returns the statement, "I understand you feel violated when I tickle you and you want me to stop. I won't do it again," he finishes, looking like a good friend.

I ask Allen, "Did it make a difference to go to your heart before you started solving this problem?" Allen and Jerod both nod. I feel an internal sign of relief. The process, of taking time to change your heart, is going to be very helpful in my classroom. It is a process of reflection, a process of refocusing energy.

Solving personal problems requires both intrapersonal and interpersonal skills. Without being in touch with ourselves, we cannot relate to the emotions of others.

NOTES

1. Barbara Kobe can be reached through Visualize, 4032 Kentucky Avenue N., Crystal, MN 55427.

2. Available from Wellness Reproductions, Inc., Beachwood, OH; 1-800-669-9208; 23945 Mercantile Road Suite KM, Beachwood, OH, 44122.

3

Emotions Affect Learning

What do we know about emotions now that differs from when you and I grew up?

First, we now know that we are always processing emotion. Every minute. Our emotions are guideposts that alert us to danger, discomfort, opportunities, joy, and peace.

Emotions distinguish us from other animals, an important development in our humanness. We are designed to seek balance. Our emotions alert us when something, internally or externally, is out of normal range. Our emotions and our intellect are not separate entities. We are one system. Wheatley and Kellner-Rogers (1996) succinctly state, "A system is an inseparable whole. It is not the sum of its parts. There is nothing to sum" (p. 72). Our physical self affects our emotions. Our emotions affect our physical self. Our thoughts affect our emotions, which affect our physical self.

What does this unity of mind, body, and emotion mean for educators? It means we are always dealing with all three. We may be focusing on the "content" of a subject, but the state of each child's emotions is ever present.

For many years, educational literature has noted the importance of an emotionally safe climate for students. A threat-

> *Emotions are not an alternative to reason, but an essential part of reason itself. If you can't feel, you can't judge. I argue that change strategies must therefore be directed more toward making schools into workplaces that recognize and support teachers' emotional relationships with their students as a vital foundation for learning, and, in the form of emotional intelligence, as a central aspect of learning itself.*
> —Andy Hargreaves (1997), *Rethinking Educational Change With Heart and Mind*, p. 3

What would life be like for adults who did not have to spend so much time getting over childhood?
—Harville Hendrix and Helen Hunt (1997), *Giving the Love That Heals*, p. 6

ening classroom, whether the adults misplan for student success or whether the teacher is insensitive to the learning needs of students' personalities, affects learning. As a child, my second-grade teacher effectively shut down my learning for 3 years. She yelled a lot; I was scared. My body-mind-spirit went into "fight or flight." I shut down in fear. My response was to become invisible. I went inside to protect myself. I hid. I froze. Forty years later, I am drawn to write about emotions as part of my search to understand that childhood experience, my frozen fears in school.

INTRAPERSONAL MORE THAN EMOTIONS

Writing in *Multiple Intelligences: The Theory in Practice,* Howard Gardner (1993) defines *Intrapersonal Intelligence* as the "knowledge of the internal aspects of a person: access to one's own feeling life, one's range of emotions, the capacity to effect discriminations among these emotions and eventually to label them and to draw upon them as a means of understanding and guiding one's own behavior" (pp. 24-25).

When Gardner first published *Frames of Mind* in 1983, the distinction between Intrapersonal and Interpersonal Intelligence was obscure for many of us. *Intrapersonal* and *interpersonal* were new concepts, contributing to new thought processes. Each personal intelligence has now developed its own aura of richness. I believe the personal intelligences are the foundations of our humanness, a strong foundation of successful learners.

Gardner's original definition focused on emotions. I believe intrapersonal intelligence includes the larger issues of self-management, including the care of our bodies. The body system supports the brain and communicates our emotions. Our emotions and our brain functioning are affected by the way we care for our bodies. As one interacting system, everything is linked—body, brain-mind, and emotions. The health of our system is affected by how we breathe and exercise, as well as what we eat. *Emotional intelligence,* a term first used by Yale University psychologist Peter Salovey and John Mayer,

Five domains of emotional intelligence, popularized by Daniel Goleman (1998):

- Knowing one's emotions—self-awareness, attention, mindfulness, able to name emotions, able to identify reasons for emotions
- Managing one's emotions—soothing oneself, calming and regaining balance, verbalizing emotions appropriately
- Motivating oneself—stifling impulsiveness, delaying gratification, maintaining focus, able to set goals and plan towards them
- Recognizing emotions in others—attuned to nonverbals, empathy, able to understand another's point of view, sensitive to other's feelings
- Handling relationships—interpersonal effectiveness, social competence, appropriate assertiveness, group decision-making strategies

was popularized in 1998 by Daniel Goleman's writing. Emotional intelligence, I believe, is a subset within the personal intelligences.

Goleman's book, *Emotional Intelligence* (1998), is filled with scientific studies related to emotion. Historically, emotions were viewed as the "dark side" of life, uncontrollable and unintelligible. Recent studies have provided insights with far-reaching significance. Emotions provide us with the most human source of information. Emotions are felt automatically and processed throughout our bodies. Emotions arouse our attention; they are at the core of our survival mechanisms. Effective processing of emotions is learned and can be taught.

In the mid-1600s, René Descartes stated, "I think, therefore I am." His writings elevated the mind—thinking—to the essence of humanness, leaving the body, the role of machinery, there to support the mind. The logic of the mind (reason) was viewed far superior to information from our body. The best minds were disembodied minds, minds without bodies. Emotions, arising from our bodies rather than reason, were therefore devalued.

Antonio Damasio, head of the Department of Neurology at the University of Iowa, challenged this 300-year-old concept in *Descartes' Error.* He wrote, "The brain and the body are indissociably integrated by mutually targeted biochemical and neural circuits" (Damasio, 1994, p. 87). Every part of the body communicates with the brain, either through the nerves, blood, or intercellular fluids. Body and brain work in concert, together.

After reading Goleman's book, I asked myself questions about emotions and my role as teacher. As teachers, what are we to make of emotions? What does the new research imply for my classroom? How do I deal with the emotions of each child in my classroom? Can I really teach emotional skills? What resources are there for teaching emotions? Do my choices of curriculum and room environment make a difference in children's emotions? What's my responsibility? What should I do?

As I read and studied, researchers and authors stimulated new insights. Stanley Greenspan (1997), in *The Growth of the Mind,* writes of his work with very young children and with autistic children. He identifies critical stages of development in our minds when our emotions, not cognitive stimulation, "serve as the mind's primary architect" (p. 7). He also challenges Descartes' concept that emotions and intellect are opposite ends of thinking. Emotions are more important, states Greenspan. Emotions "create, organize, and orchestrate many of the mind's most important functions" (p. 7). "Unlikely as the scenario may seem," Greenspan writes, "emotions are in fact the architects of a vast array of cognitive operations throughout the life span. Indeed, they make possible all creative thought" (p. 7). Emotions shape our intellect. Emotions focus our attention, link our experiences, and guide our intentions, which affects the activities we choose.

All experiences are linked to emotional overtones. Sensory experiences, such as light, are processed by physical properties (bright or dim) and also the emotional meaning we bring to them (jarring or unsafe). Experiences are always linked with their emotional qualities. When the meaning is safe or neutral, we simply file the experience without much thought. But the experience still has an emotional component. Greenspan explains that this double-coding system allows us to "cross-reference" each memory. It is emotions that give experiences meaning and relevance. Every experience imprints both a sensory memory and emotional memory. They are bonded together. *Neurons that fire together wire together.*

Different aspects of the memory are stored in different areas of the brain and the body. Remembering an experience brings back the emotions of that time. We feel this emotion throughout our bodies, in our smiles, in our stomachs, backs, and necks. Our emotions show in the way we walk, slump, or stand tall. There is no specific neuron that remembers my grandmother's loving smile. I remember her by recreating all of the different sensory memories, integrated with my present experiences.

> *Emotions and bodily sensations are intricately intertwined, in a bidirectional network in which each can alter the other.... These recent discoveries are important for appreciating how memories are stored not only in the brain, but in a psychosomatic network extending into the body.*
> —Candace Pert (1997), *Molecules of Emotion,* p. 142 and p. 143

Each experience is affected by the memories of the past and their connected emotions. This is why it is so critical that my students experience positive emotions in my classroom. Learning is bonded with emotions. Often, parents who had negative school experiences find it difficult to attend school conferences. For these parents, their memories of school and feeling bad about themselves are still bonded many years later.

DISCRIMINATION METER

Our emotions organize our experiences and our behaviors. Consider how a young child decides when to say "hello." She isn't given a set of rules—say hello to everyone who is family, or lives in our neighborhood, or to everyone. Greenspan explains, each of us develops a "discrimination meter" based on complex social clues and we figure out that we "say hello when you feel friendly toward someone." The simple act of saying hello is based on the emotional cues within. Emotions are the organizing factor.

> *We can no longer afford to ignore the emotional origins of intelligence.*
> —Stanley Greenspan (1997), *The Growth of the Mind,* p. 40

Our "discrimination meter" constantly scans the environment picking up the nonverbals that register emotionally and guide our behaviors.

The emotional brain scans everything happening to us from moment to moment, to see if something that happened in the past that made us sad or angry is like what is happening now. If so, the amygdala calls an alarm—to declare an emergency and mobilize in a split second to act. And it can do so, in brain time, more rapidly than the thinking brain takes to figure out what is going on, which is why people can get into a rage and do something very inappropriate that they wished they hadn't. It's an emotional hijacking.

—Daniel Goleman in "Up With Emotional Health," *Educational Leadership*, pp. 12-13

"Our ability to discriminate and generalize," Greenspan (1997) writes, "stems from the fact that we carry inside us as we go from one situation to another the emotions that automatically tell us what to say, do, and even think" (p. 25).

Before every action we rapidly consult our memories of past physical and emotional experiences. Instantly, we determine the meaning of an event and possible actions based on our previous experiences. Our emotions sort and organize our experiences. Only then do we use thinking to evaluate our ideas and life events. Thinking is the logical analysis of emotionally driven ideas. Our emotions create our "islands of explanation" about what is safe; our intellect puts them into a logical framework.

Rather than being considered less than intellect, emotions are now recognized as the organizing force. Emotions come first, the input before any analysis. Yesterday in my classroom, I motioned to Joseph, asking him to come out of the class meeting to talk with me. He protested loudly, "I didn't do anything, you're always picking on me!!!" Emotions. Emotions before analysis. Joseph merely needed to go down to the school office to deal with an attendance issue.

DEVELOPMENTAL ISSUES

Immediately after birth, a child's neurons begin a three-year period of rapid dendrite branching. In the metaphoric language of Marian Diamond, the "magic trees of the mind" are developing. This developmental period has spurts of activity recorded by EEGs. In the first three years of life, there are six peaks of electrical activity. (There are another six peaks in the years before age 30.) During this period, a child's brain organizes sensory experiences. In infancy, sounds may be stimulat-

Figure 3.1. Artist's Rendering of Rapid Dendrite Branching at Three Ages of Development.

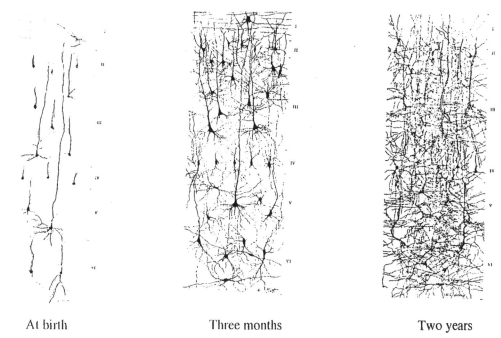

| At birth | Three months | Two years |

SOURCE: Diamond and Hopson (1998, pp. 106-107).

ing the visual cortex as well as the auditory cortex. This is labeled synesthesia. Sights may stimulate the touch cortex. The brain is not pre-wired before birth. *Experiences wire the brain.* The brain searches for patterns emerging from a confusing milieu of stimulation. Sights become images. Repeated images become memories. Mother's face and mother's smell become bonded to a satisfying sense of food. Through experiences and sensations, a child begins to organize its brain into the patterns we know as the occipital lobe (vision), the parietal lobe (touch and movement), the temporal lobe (hearing), and the frontal lobe. The frontal lobe, responsible for conscious decision making, continues to develop for 30 years.

The infant's initial task is to make order out of the many sensations in her body. Too little stimulation slows this process. Too much stimulation overwhelms the process. The child must learn to manage the sensations and decipher what needs attention. This new brain must learn that *this* sound (the telephone ringing) is OK so don't pay attention, versus *that* sound (mother yelling in fear) is not OK and pay attention right now. This is the beginning of focused attention.

> A small child knows how others will react to her not because she can think about it logically but because her emotions, linked into extensive patterns based on experience, tell her about closeness, about assertiveness, about sexuality, about frustration, about what leads to acceptance and what leads to fear or pain.
> —Stanley Greenspan (1997), *The Growth of the Mind*, p. 73

For reasons not yet understood, some people grow up without mastering this attention-sorting process. Some people experience normal sounds very loudly. Their auditory system becomes confused by such sounds. Others find "normal" lighting too bright. Some are extremely sensitive to touch. A boy in my class is touch sensitive. His mother must cut the label tags off his clothes because the labels irritate him, distracting him. His brain did not wire up in a "normal" pattern to organize sensory stimulation.

Emotions are linked to the infant's experiences during the process of wiring up, the connecting of the dendrites of their sensory brains. The youngster has no consciousness at this time. She has no words, yet she experiences an intense emotional life. The amygdala, processing fear, functions early in life. Emotions are explicitly linked to experiences.

Organizing sensory stimulation and the beginnings of attention are the first stages of emotional development. In the second stage, humans begin to fall in love—the parent-child interplay of love. The parent coos and smiles. She rocks the infant, and the infant begins to notice pleasure, an emotion. Communication between parent and child begins. The baby glows with a sense of love. As we've witnessed with the Romanian orphans in dire institutional settings, without the love and attention of caring adults, children simply do not thrive. The capacity for human closeness, for intimacy, begins with infant experiences.

During the first year of life babies learn willful behavior. Greenspan identifies this behavior as the beginnings of "who I am" versus "the other I want to influence." Wanting to influence carries the emotions of desire and also intention. This is a new level of consciousness. New brain pathways are required to deal with subtle social clues—winks, laughs, playful nonverbal dialogues. During these dialogues, if the child doesn't get

what he wants, he experiences frustration and anger. It is too soon for the baby to consciously hold
an idea, but it is not too early to register emotional qualities.

Between 12 and 18 months the child uses
his sensory experiences and emotion of intent to develop purposeful interactions.
This is a crucial bridge to healthy emotional development. The child wants to go
outside, so she pulls the adult to the
door. The child wants a snack. She
points, and the parent provides. Nonverbally, the child puzzles out what
works to get what she wants. This
is intention. It is purposeful interaction. The child (ideally) learns
that her "wants" are taken seriously. An incredible richness of
emotional experiences are happening in the process. Young-
sters have begun to understand nonverbals. They are figuring
out strategies for getting their desires met. The child has begun to learn what is acceptable and unacceptable in her family's culture. All of this emotional interplay is vital for further
learning. These emotions define what is safe and what can be
explored. Unfortunately, children whose parents do not respond, due to depression, lack of energy, or other reasons, may
not learn these beginning lessons of socialization.

The common origins of emotions and intellect demand a conception of intelligence that integrates those mental processes that have been traditionally described as cognitive and those qualities that have been described as emotional, including the sense of self or the ego, the awareness of reality, conscience, the capacity for reflection, and the like. The mind's most important faculties are rooted in emotional experiences from very early in life—before even the earliest awareness of symbols, conscious or unconscious.
—Stanley Greenspan, *The Growth of the Mind,* p. 40

At this point, the child has collected enough sensory emotional experiences to mentally "picture" a similar experience.
This picturing is the beginning of conscious abstract thought.
It is the beginning of thinking. The child has begun to understand that pictures represent the real thing. The child has
enough stored experience to begin imaginative play. Now the
child is able to translate emotions to his teddy bear: "Teddy
feels sad because . . ." A tremendous amount of emotional material has been processed to this point. Here are the beginnings of
empathy.

This ability to translate emotions, to think about emotions,
also leads to the beginnings of reflection. It leads to the ability
to think about why we feel as we do. This is not a simple task. I

The skills that Henry needs to learn in school, and that would make it possible for him to reach his true intellectual potential, are not innate characteristics but proficiencies that can be taught. Indeed they are nothing more than the skills acquired at the developmental levels. First, a child must be able to regulate his attention. Whether he learns this easily or with difficulty depends, of course, on the particular endowment he arrived with as well as the early nurturing he received. Second, he must be able to relate to others with warmth and trust. Those who lack adequate nurturing may not have learned to engage fully with other human beings. No teacher can then marshal this basic sense of connectedness. The child will not be motivated to please her, and ultimately himself, by doing well at schoolwork. Finally, he must be able to communicate through both gestures and symbols, to handle complex ideas, and to make connections among them. Those who have not mastered these early levels obviously cannot succeed at more advanced ones. The real ABCs come down to attention, strong relationships, and communication, all of which children must learn through interactions with adults.
—Stanley Greenspan (1997), *The Growth of the Mind*, p. 220

work extensively on reflection in my classroom. The Stephen Covey business training uses reflection extensively. Many adults still strive to understand "why we feel as we do."

At this young age, the child begins to learn that she can alter her emotions by thinking. For instance, by remembering sitting on grandma's loving lap, the child feels better. "I liked sitting on Grandma's lap. I hope she comes again soon." In the process, the child is learning a sense of past, present, and future.

Emotions and intention drive our attention. Being able to focus one's attention is crucial for success in school. Feeling powerful enough to shape one's life is crucial for trying new things, for making plans, and for self-evaluation. These factors normally develop during most children's early years. Unfortunately, each year I meet children who have not developed attentional focus—a skill critical to academic success.

THE BIOLOGY OF EMOTIONS

Candace Pert (1997) offers a clear explanation of the chemistry of our emotions. Peptide molecules, the physical representation of our emotions, are spread throughout our bodies. Peptides are abundant within our midbrain where the amygdala, hippocampus, and hypothalamus are located. These same peptides are also abundant in our stomachs, identified as "gut feelings," and other body areas. Pert explains, "These biochemicals are the physiological substrates of emotion, the molecular underpinnings of what we experience as feelings, sensations, thoughts, drives, perhaps even spirit or soul" (p. 130). Emotions are our alert system.

Many years ago, Charles Darwin realized that people over the world use the same facial expressions for similar emotions. He pondered the meaning of this physiology, developed over eons, and speculated that emotions are a key to survival. *Emotions are now understood to be the highest level of biological feedback.* Candace Pert (1997) explains,

> We can no longer think of the emotions as having less validity than physical, material substance, but instead must see them as cellular signals that are involved in the process of translating information into physical reality, literally transforming mind into matter. Emotions are at the nexus between matter and mind, going back and forth between the two and influencing both. (p. 189)

We need joy—it flushes our biological system with health. We need anger—it provides clues to define our boundaries. We need fear—it alerts us to danger. Emotions provide critical information for our survival.

Growing up in the 1950s, my family culture taught me to express only middle-of-the-road emotions. If I felt very sad, I was expected to go to my room and come out with a smiling face when I was over it. It was not OK to express sadness about the ordinary trial and tribulations of growing up. It also was not OK to run and jump for joy. When I was very happy, I was expected to remain ladylike and calm. Thus, I learned not to listen to the emotional messages from my body.

Why are some people more in touch with emotions than others are? Why are some people ruled by their emotions, or hijacked by emotions? Pert (1997) writes,

> All sensory information undergoes a filtering process as it travels across one or more synapses, eventually (but not always) reaching the areas of higher processes, like the frontal lobes. There the sensory input—concerning the view, the odor, the caress—enters our conscious awareness. The efficiency of the filtering process, which chooses what stimuli we pay attention to at any given moment, is determined by the quantity and quality of the receptors at

The work of Candace Pert (1997), now Research Professor in Physiology and Biophysics at Georgetown University Medical Center in Washington, D.C., has focused on the "molecules of emotions" floating throughout our bodies. She explains that typical neurons have millions of receptor molecules on their surfaces. Receptor molecules are chains of amino acids, proteins, which function as scanners, each looking for the right molecular combination. The receptor molecules

> cluster in the cellular membrane waiting for the right chemical keys to swim up to them through the extracellular fluid and to mount them by fitting into their keyholes—a process known as *binding*.
>   Binding. It's *sex* on a molecular level!
>   And what is this chemical key that docks onto the receptor and causes it to dance and sway? This responsible element is called a *ligand*. This is the chemical key that binds to the receptor, entering it like a key in a keyhole, creating a disturbance to tickle the molecule into rearranging itself, changing its shape until—click!— information enters the cell. (Pert, 1997, p. 23)

"These minute physiological phenomena at the cellular level can translate to large changes in behavior, physical activity, even mood" (Pert, 1997, p. 24). The molecular process is very selective. Exactly the right key (ligand) must drift by the right keyhole (receptor) in order to communicate.

> There are three major types of ligands. Neurotransmitters are the smallest; they pass information across the synapse, which is the minute gap between neurons. Dopamine, histamine, serotonin, acetylcholine, norepinephrine and GABA are this type of ligand. Steroids are the second type of ligand.
>   Natural steroids begin as cholesterol and become transformed into hormones such as testosterone, progesterone, estrogen, and cortisol. The third type, peptides, make up 95% of the ligands. These peptides are the 'molecules of emotion.' (Pert, 1997, p. 27)

When Pert wrote *Molecules of Emotion* (1997), 88 different peptides had been identified.

> Receptors and their ligands have come to be seen as 'information molecules'—the basic units of a language used by cells throughout the organism to communicate across systems such as the endocrine, neurological, gastro-intestinal, and even the immune system. (Pert, 1997, p. 27)

> This is revolutionary research—research that Pert had trouble publishing for years because of the mindset that the neurons-synapse system was the core communication system of the brain. This system, the brain's neuron-axon-dendrite-synapse-neurotransmitter system, is now referred to as the brain's electrical communication system. The peptides circulate through blood and cerebrospinal fluid (the "extracellular space") is referred to as the chemical brain.

these nodal points. The relative quantities and qualities of these receptors are determined by many things, among them your experiences yesterday and as a child, even by what you ate for lunch today. (p. 142)

We are the net whole of all of our life—our genetics, our experiences, our food, and our thoughts. Our emotional quality is affected by all of these. We are a psychosomatic network, an integrated network of our thoughts, our emotions, and our bodies. We are one whole body, mind, and spirit system.

THE HIGH ROAD AND LOW ROAD

Joseph LeDoux (1996) explains the biology of our emotional processing has two pathways—the High Road and the Low Road. The path of the Low Road, labeled by Daniel Goleman as *emotional hijacking,* travels directly from the sensory thalamus to the amygdala, which is the major processing center for emotions. This is the "act now and think later" pathway. The body acts, or rather reacts, with great speed. The amygdala taps into past experiences, overgeneralizes, and tends to assume the worst. Young children's behavior represents the Low Road—reaction without thinking.

Figure 3.2. The Chemical Influences on Attention and Behavior

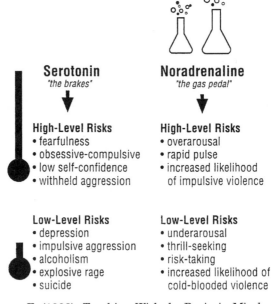

SOURCE: From Jensen, E. (1998). *Teaching With the Brain in Mind,* p. 76. Alexandria, VA: Association for Supervision and Curriculum Development. Copyright ©1998 ASCD. Reprinted by permission. All rights reserved.

Note: The levels indicated are high or low compared to the norm. Generally, males have 20-40% lower serotonin levels than females. Human behavior is complex, and there are other influencing factors besides chemical inbalances.

REFLECTIVE AND REFLEXIVE

Robert Sylwester (1997b) refers to the Low Road as the "fast, reflexive response system." Unfortunately, I see more and more students who are reflexive. They react at the least provocation. An accidental brush of an arm is enough for the student to react in a fighting posture. This is the dominant approach of students whose home or neighborhood environment is dangerous. This is the approach of children who have learned to hit first, and hit hard, if someone threatens you. It is the emotional root of senseless violence. This trigger behavior also stimulates the increase of cortisol, a peptide molecule that activates other stress chemicals.

One reason that aggressive youths tend to mellow as they get older, researchers suspect, is that serotonin levels increase with age. And the reason that females generally are less aggressive than males may be because their serotonin levels are 20 to 30 percent higher.

A low serotonin level also can dry up the wellsprings of life's happiness, withering a person's interest in his existence and increasing the risk of depression and suicide. Alcoholism, sleeplessness, sexual deviance, fire-setting, obesity, and other impulse-control disorders also have been laid at the doorstep of low serotonin.

A growing body of evidence indicates that low levels of serotonin are implicated in a lack of control, the kind of behavior that typically manifests itself as irritability, loss of temper, and explosive rage. It is the type of impulsive aggression that is escalating at an unprecedented pace in the United States.

While the U.S. population increased by 40 percent from 1960 through 1991, violent crime increased by 560 percent, murders increased 170 percent, rapes 520 percent, and aggravated assaults 600 percent, according to the FBI.

—(Kotulak, 1996, pp. 60-61)

The reflexive response is designed for immediate, threatening danger—a car is speeding toward you—but is destructive as a way of life. High cortisol levels make it difficult for an individual to distinguish between a real threat and a lesser encounter. Chronically high cortisol levels destroy the hippocampus neurons necessary for memory and learning. When a small child experiences repeated reflexive aggression, his normal aggression set point, like body temperature, is altered. The developing brain creates a set point for serotonin, the calming-down or "braking system," which is lower than normal, and a higher set point for noradrenaline. Noradrenaline, which produces adrenaline, is the "alarm hormone," increasing the tendency for violence.

The second path, the emotional High Road, sends emotional messages to the frontal lobes for processing before it goes to the fear-oriented amygdala. This route takes longer, but this process evaluates input and makes a plan. Brain pathways for the High Road develop over time, according to one's life experiences and cultural expectations. Sylwester refers to the High Road as the "slow, reflective response system." It is this frontal lobe pathway I intend to develop as I teach children about emotions, stress, goal setting, and planning. Positive emotional response, such as recognizing others' emotions, and productive interpersonal communication are skills developed through experiences of the slower, reflective response system. Planning and persistence are learned, frontal lobe, reflective response-abilities.

Many connections exist between the amygdala and the frontal lobes; it is a virtual one-way superhighway. Unfortunately, significantly fewer connections exist from the cerebral cortex back to the amygdala. Joseph LeDoux likened this path to a rural back road. The difference between the roads makes it harder for "thinking" to affect emotions and easy for emotions to dominate thinking.

Unconscious memories are processed by the amygdala, which is the first alert system for our fear response. Conscious memories, processed by the hippocampus, are evaluated only by the reflective system. The difference between the two roads is particularly relevant as we plan experiences for developmental levels of the children in our care. We cannot afford to hope children will happen to learn these skills. We must deliberately plan to teach personal emotional skills.

The two pathways serve two distinct purposes. The quick, reflexive Low Road is critical for life-threatening events, for survival. It is a very important system, but primitive. In today's world we must develop the reflective, High Road processing that enables children to use positive intrapersonal self-management skills.

4

Personal Intelligences
Across Curriculum

A number of curriculum programs are designed to teach the social-emotional goals of Intrapersonal and Interpersonal Intelligences. I believe in a direct skill-based focus, but that is only a small part of teaching for personal intelligences. Intrapersonal and interpersonal skills are enmeshed throughout my curriculum. I hope teachers will recognize the implications of their curricular choices in relation to the personal intelligences.

SYMBOLIC MESSAGES

During a Project Zero Seminar at Harvard, David Perkins elaborated on the idea of functional and symbolic messages. His metaphor increased my awareness of related classroom issues, bringing further clarity to my classroom practices. An organization's functional messages are represented by its structure and goals. In schools there is a head, the principal, and teachers running classrooms of children. It is a functional hierarchical structure. The symbolic message of a hierarchy is one of lesser or greater authority (knowledge, intelligence, wisdom), with the children on the bottom. In any organization

> Enormous cognitive growth can emerge from the social interactions of students throughout the school day: rich, textured, thoughtful teaching between learners who care about each other's ideas and are interested in bouncing their own off the nearest sounding board. The more carefully a classroom is structured to allow for such productive social engagement, the more academic growth will emerge.
> —Chip Wood (1999), *Time to Teach, Time to Learn*, p. 163

there are functional structures that carry implied symbolic messages. Calling on the "bright" children carries an obvious symbolic message.

I began reflecting on the symbolic messages classroom environments may be giving children, particularly in relation to the personal intelligences. Are there practices in our schools that carry implied messages that children should not notice their emotions? Are there messages about achievement? Are there messages that imply the teacher is the only one who should be making decisions and controlling children's thoughts?

My intention is to convey symbolic messages that encourage self-awareness, choice and decision making, self-monitoring, and effective handing of relationships. Our morning meeting begins with a thought for the day, discussion, and sharing. At the end of the meeting I ask, "What are you going to start on today?" There are many choices during each week's activities. The assignments are clear, but broad enough to accommodate the diversity of skill levels.

By asking, instead of directing, I encourage each child to evaluate her possibilities, become aware of her priorities and feelings, and make a decision. My goal is to get my students into their own purposeful intrinsic learning. I want them to work on projects with depth of thought, not an eye to the clock. I want their brains turned on.

TWO-HOUR WORK BLOCKS

My classroom environment is very different from the traditional classroom of my early teaching days. In that classroom, times were listed for each subject, and we all worked on that subject together. My old way, symbolically, gave the message that a student's feelings at the moment were irrelevant. I didn't trust children to be able to make decisions regarding the order or time they spent on specific projects. Now, my morning is a two-hour work block, giving the symbolic message that I have confidence my students can handle choices. It carries the mes-

One week's assignments:

4 pages of math—2 Wed., 2 Fri.
Spelling: Mon. list, Wed. practice, Fri. test
Prepare for History Group presentations—Tues. & Thurs.
Sketch microscopic slides—2 dry mounts Wed., 2 wet mounts Fri.
3rd and final copy of your long, scary story—Thurs.
Weights of shells on triple balance, using grams—Wed.
Draw your hand with wrinkle details—Thurs.

sage that it is important to make choices and learn to manage your time.

CLASS RECORD BOOK

In any classroom, records of children's accomplishments must be accurately kept. In our classroom, the record book is always on the central counter so any child, or parent, can discuss progress with me. Open records encourage student's self-monitoring. Most fifth graders need to learn self-monitoring. To learn these skills they have to have the opportunity to practice these skills. Some students need more coaching than others to successfully complete their work. In the first months of our school year, I often ask such questions as, "Do you know what assignments you need to do? Have you checked the record book? What are your priorities today?"

My record system is fairly simple. There is a "Turn In Papers" tray. As I mark in papers, I put like assignments together in a folder. If a paper isn't of the quality I'd expect, I conference with the child to find the difficulty and strategize for a higher level of success. During a class meeting, I may pass out the papers in a folder for further discussion. For instance, when children collected information on what they ate for a week, it was valuable to discuss that information as a group. The point was made that some children were not eating from the six food groups appropriately.

Another benefit of the work folders is immediate access to the work when a child says, "I turned that in." I simply hand the child the folder and say non-judgmentally, "This is what I

It is extremely important to have conversations with children about mistakes. When Edison was asked if he felt bad about the thousands of things he tried before he figured out the electric light, he said something to the effect that those weren't mistakes, they were opportunities to learn. "Mistakes are opportunities to learn," I explain to the children. "If people weren't trying something new, they would probably not make mistakes because they would know exactly what to do. In our classroom we all will make mistakes. I hope you will just learn from your mistakes and go on." I make lots of mistakes in front of the children. Somehow my brain confuses the names of children when they begin with the same letter—like Kaelyn and Kyndra, two children about as different as they can be. During the first days of school we discuss "making mistakes" and I share my saying, "First mistake of the year!" It works great on the mistakes I make the first week, and all through the year. In May, I'm still saying, "First mistake of the year!" as the children laugh. It's important to be comfortable with our mistakes.

Those of us who teach are often tolerant of students' mistakes—especially when we believe that the students are of limited intelligence—but it does not occur to us to view their answers not as mistakes, but as responses to a different context. When we are mindful, we recognize that every inadequate answer is adequate in another context.
—Ellen Langer (1997), *The Power of Mindful Learning,* p. 135

have, check to see if I've made a mistake." Sometimes I have made a mistake. But sometimes the work is not in the folder. Then I suggest, "Why not check the No-Names Papers under the Turn-In tray." Most often, the child will find his or her paper. This process of sorting student papers deliberately involves the child. If teachers throw away 'no-name papers,' children have no evidence to help them learn better self-management. Eventually, all papers are sorted into portfolios.

Over time, students become better at determining what they should do as homework (because it is "easy" for them) and what they need to do at school (because they need help from the teacher or need to use school materials). Choices make it easier to learn self-motivation. Choices are especially important for students who don't come to school well motivated. We learn to make good decisions by making decisions and reflecting on whether the decision gave the desired results.

In my classroom, children complete each assignment. I monitor for their success. Yet, there are important, subtle differences between a teacher "making" children do assignments and monitoring for success. I don't "keep" students after school if their work is not done, but I do "offer" an hour of extra help if children want to stay after school. I don't "keep" children in from recess, but some ask, "Could I stay in and finish this project? I'll be real quiet," and I "allow" them the extra time. I want children to assume responsibility for their success. How I set up systems, and the words I use, convey distinctively different messages from the traditional classroom management I used earlier in my career. Sometimes I say to a child, "No, I don't think that decision is appropriate because you have this late work to finish." Yes, there is a bottom line—I require my students to turn in all of their assignments before they can participate in a school roller-skating event. Some children don't believe that I will stick to this bottom line. Maybe adults in their lives have not followed through on consequences. Some children whine to parents or claim, "no fair." But, the roller-skating event is publicized for weeks and I stick to my expectation. Children rise to the occasion and are proud of themselves as they put in the extra effort to complete every assignment with good quality.

> We ourselves have never experienced any school learning that is not social and emotional in its implications and consequences. The process of being schooled delivers social and emotional messages to a student in everything from the route of a school bus through end-of-day glimpses of school custodians cleaning up the building. Classroom decorations, student behavior in corridors, homework assignments, textbooks, and the minute-by-minute body language of teachers and students carry embedded and various social and emotional messages.
> —Peggy McIntosh and Emily Style (1999), "Social, Emotional, and Political Learning," in *Educating Minds and Hearts*, p. 137

Traditionally, a symbolic message is the expectation that all children at a specific grade level are on the same page of the math textbook (spelling textbook, social studies textbook, etc.). Eleven-year-olds are incredibly different in their skill levels, their prior knowledge, their motivation, and their attention. The everyone-on-the-same-page classroom sends the message that children "should be alike."

I spend weeks in the beginning of the year developing the concept that each of us have different, multiple intelligences, just as we have different hair and facial features. Each child is unique. How do "should be alike" messages affect children's awareness of who they really are, and how they feel? The everyone-on-the-same-page classroom does not reflect personal uniqueness. It may, instead, foster feelings of competition where there is little sensitivity to others' feelings. Obviously, the symbolic message is that some children are "better" on the same page than others, creating a hierarchy of smartness instead of valuing our diversity. My multi-age classroom, without textbooks, helps break down the expectation that children should be alike. Children of similar age come with extreme diversity.

FRIENDLY HELPERS

Once a week, for a half hour, my students are Friendly Helpers for children in a first- and second-grade class. Each student is paired with a younger student for the full school year. They befriend the child, getting to know the child's interests and skills. For the first few weeks, my students read to their younger partner and the younger student reads to my students. There is time to talk and share. My students interview their younger partners to determine skill levels in rhyming, initial sounds, beginning words, writing, simple addition and subtraction, and reading numbers. This serves as a planning guide for my students as they figure out what to teach the younger children. We discuss what makes a good helper. I reteach my students how to use math manipulatives with children. We brainstorm word families they can teach to their younger partners. I pass along ideas that worked for me when I taught first and second graders. Sometimes, the teacher of the first and second graders asks my students to assist with a class project, such as paper weaving or clay boats. These projects are more successful with older friends' helping hands, which support the young person's success.

The design of my ideal school of the future is based upon two assumptions. The first is that not all people have the same interests and abilities; not all of us learn in the same way. (And we now have the tools to begin to address these individual differences in school.) The second assumption is one that hurts: it is the assumption that nowadays no one person can learn everything there is to learn.
—Howard Gardner (1993),
Multiple Intelligences, p. 10

When I asked the first and second graders what was good about having a Friendly Helper, they replied: "She helps me." "Mike is nice, he's fun to work with." "My friend draws really good." One child explained, "And he's on my bus too!" There is a sense of safety being connected to an older child, and a sense of being valued by a younger child.

Some days my students complain that the younger child isn't cooperating. I respond, "I know how that feels as a teacher. What do you think you can do to get better cooperation?" We spend some time in reflective problem solving, and I make a note to check on this pair next week. The reflection on Friendly Helpers days consists of recording what the pair worked on and how the child reacted and planning for the next time together. "What worked well? What was hard?" The reflection, the planning, and the relationship benefit the development of my students just as much as nurturing the younger students The symbolic message of valuing another, listening, and contributing to another's growth is a significant message.

> In fact, some scholars have argued that of all the methods recommended in the last decade for improving education, cross-age tutoring generates the largest gains in learning for the least financial cost.
> —Charles Fisher and David Berliner (1995), *Perspectives on Instructional Time*, p. 308

HEALTHY BODIES INFLUENCE BRAINS

Fifth and sixth graders are ready to increase their responsibility for making decisions about their bodies. Most have basic habits of self-care, although some come to school disheveled and dirty. This is an important time; lifelong self-management habits relating to food and exercise are being developed. In my classroom, many children are not aware of the effect food and exercise has on their brains. They are mired in short-term enjoyment and immediate gratification. Habits of food and exercise are within the context of the self-awareness and self-management domain of Intrapersonal Intelligence.

My district's standards for health education include reading food labels, understanding the pyramid of the six food groups, naming a healthy diet, and understanding the effects of food on emotions and brain power.

I begin with a pretest to assess my students' understanding of nutrition issues, linking to their prior knowledge—what they know, feel, and understand.

What Do You Know?

What foods would make a balanced breakfast? Explain why.

Fill in the food triangle with food groups and optimal number of daily servings.

What is your favorite food? Why?

How much exercise do you get each week? Why is exercise important?

Name the major body systems.

Explain two ways body systems interconnect.

In a 1998 study, doctors at Massachusetts General Hospital tracked 100 third through eighth graders who ate, or didn't eat, school breakfast. Frequent breakfasters had fewer absences, behaved better, and averaged higher math scores. The breakfasts in the study consisted of bread/muffin or cereal, milk, and fruit. Eating a decent breakfast is important for brain power.

The breakfasts used in this study were good quality. Unfortunately, what I see in school breakfasts is not always good quality. I find it hard to believe Fruit Loops cereal and a chocolate-covered doughnut is a balanced breakfast, but those foods are in our school breakfasts. Unfortunately, it is often the poorest children, those least likely to have good nutrition at home, who eat our school breakfasts. I see the effects of poor nutrition in my classroom. Allen gets cranky and out of sorts. Steffi's mind wanders and her learning energy plummets.

> *All receptors are proteins . . . they cluster in the cellular membrane waiting for the right chemical keys to swim up to them through the extracellular fluid.*
> —Candace Pert (1997), *Molecules of Emotion*, p. 23

Children need breakfasts with adequate protein and complex carbohydrates to maintain their alertness. Working with stomach enzymes, proteins release 21 amino acids. One of those, tyrosine, turns into dopamine. "The dopamine circuit is the heart of the reward system," writes Ronald Kotulak (1996, p. 116). Positive school experiences rely on the chemistry of dopamine. Tyrosine also stimulates amino acids, which stimulate the attentiveness and alertness students need in school. Proteins are crucial for good brain functioning. Adequate protein for children, according to Marion Diamond, who has conducted numerous protein studies, is at least two servings of fish, poultry, lean meat, eggs, nuts, or beans daily as well as three to four servings of dairy products.

No knowledge is more crucial than knowledge about health. Without it, no other life goal can be successfully achieved.
—Ernest Boyer (1983), *High School*, p. 304

In 1994, child nutrition was studied in a USDA report. The assistant secretary for the Food and Consumer Services stated that the study revealed "government-sponsored school meals served to kids today do not meet the government's own nutritional standards for a healthful diet" (Given, 1998, p. 71). Eleven children in my class depend on school breakfast and lunch. For some children the food may be the most nutritious of the day, even though it's less than they deserve to facilitate their best learning power.

Our brains float in fluid and must have water to function effectively. As children become dehydrated, they lose attentiveness, often without being conscious that they are dehydrated. Good tasting, cool water is a necessity for children's brains. I invite parents to help pay for the five-gallon, bottled spring water dispenser in our classroom. Children bring a cup to school, with their name on it, for reuse. We all drink water throughout the day. Before tests, I encourage children to have a number of glasses of water near them so they can drink frequently, even if they can't walk over to the water urn.

BODY SYSTEMS

The importance of water and appropriate food habits are definitely included as I teach about the human body. To begin our body study, I put up a large chart paper covering the length of the chalkboard. "What's one body system you know about?" I ask.

Hands wave, "Our blood system, what's it called?"

"Circulatory system. The circulatory system bathes our bodies in water and carries the chemistry needed for all the processes of our bodies. What body parts are involved in the circulatory system?"

Poor health interferes with learning; good health facilitates it.
—Eva Marx and Susan Frelick Wooley (1998), *Health Is Academic*, p. 17

I continue to probe until all "systems" are identified. Then I pose a problem: "The respiratory system also interacts with the circulatory system, so are they separate systems?" As children recognize the overlaps, I draw lines connecting the body part labels, illustrating the interrelationships of our body systems. During the next two weeks, cooperative groups will prepare to teach the class about the systems and their interrelationships. Children will do demonstrations and measuring activities, watch videos, and conduct experiments designed to teach the rest of the class about their body systems.

RESEARCH REPORTS

Even research reports carry subtle symbolic messages. Each fall, my students learn research skills by studying famous people. We begin with student pairs brainstorming all the famous people they know in a fun, timed competition. Pairs count their total number of famous people and the winner is declared. Then I ask students to count how many people of color are on their lists and another winning pair is identified. I ask the groups to further classify if the people are identified with Native American, Hispanic, Asian, or black culture. Next, we count for women and declare yet another winning group. "Why," I ask, "do you know so little about people of color and women?" Their reflections are accurate—issues of racism, sexism, and respect. Finally, I refer to a chart of Gardner's eight intelligences and ask groups to categorize the names under the appropriate intelligence.

When the children's charts are posted, we can easily see the results. Children know a lot about entertainers, both musical and kinesthetic. "All entertainers together are less than 1% of the jobs in our world. It's obvious that you know a lot of entertainers. For your research report you can't study an entertainer unless he/she is also famous for something special, like Jackie Robinson. What was special about Jackie Robinson?" I ask.

Smart classrooms shift the emphasis from teaching to learning. Education is what takes place in the minds of the students. In smart schools the teacher does not do the learning any more than a coach scores goals or shoots baskets. He or she is the facilitator, the manager of instructions, who creates the proper learning context and helps the student to take responsibility for his or her own learning."
—Edward Fiske (1991), *Smart Schools, Smart Kids,* p. 66

What is the symbolic message in this process? Reflect on how different the symbolic message would be if I asked students to write their reports on a U.S. president—all white males. This assignment, to learn research skills by studying a famous person, honors the diversity of all of my students. It is a message of inclusion. This year the children's report topics included Charles Drew, Clara Barton, Cesar Chavez, Sacajawea, Rosa Parks, Albert Einstein, Wilma Rudolph, Georgia O'Keefe, among others.

> Every young person has a deep need to belong. Children with the greatest unmet needs for relationships are often those most alienated from adults and peers. Schools and youth work programs must make a planned and concerted effort to nourish inviting relationships in a culture of belonging.
> —Larry Brendtro, Martin Brokenleg, and Steve Van Bockern (1990), *Reclaiming Youth at Risk*, p. 69

As we progress through the steps of making note cards and organizing cards for topic sentences for their reports, I model what the children will need to do to teach the class about their famous person. "I am going to model a report presentation. I'll explain what I've learned about Nelson Mandela. I won't read the information. I'll use eye contact and show you 'stuff' to make it interesting." I begin by asking children to share what they already know about Mandela, linking to their prior knowledge to engage their brains. One child knows Mandela was the first Black president of South Africa. I pull down the map and we locate South Africa. Another child shares, "He is kind of like Martin Luther King. He fought for equal rights."

"Who were the original people of South Africa?"

"Black Africans."

"Then why weren't they running the country?" The conversation takes a side journey for an analogy about the United States. I have Native American children in my class and it is especially important they understand this. "Who were the original people on our continent?" I ask.

Stacey speaks up, "My people and Jerod's, the Native peoples."

"Yes, and what happened?" The colonization of North America and South Africa has many similarities. We dwell on it a while and return to thinking about South Africa. "In South Africa, black people were not slaves, but the government developed laws to keep them from having power. Talk to a person next to you about what kind of laws a government could make that would keep a group of people from having power."

Education is the great engine of personal development. It is what we make out of what we have, not what we are given, that separates one person from another.
—Nelson Mandela (1994), *Long Walk to Freedom*, p. 194

The room tunes to the buzz of voices. "I don't know the answer," complains one child.

"I want you to invent an answer. What do you think? Be creative. What would keep you from growing up in power?" Problem solving, putting oneself in another's shoes, relating personally to history—these are my goals.

We reconvene as a group. I'm ready to list ideas on the chalkboard. Tim shares, "You could make a law that they can't be citizens."

That pretty well sums it up, but I continue. "Does that mean you can vote?"

"No!"

"Will the government provide good schools for you?"

"No."

"Will you be able to get good-paying jobs?" I continue to make points. My students begin to feel the unfairness of South Africa's apartheid policies. I am connecting their emotions with historical events and building empathy.

I begin the story of Mandela's life. As a young boy, Nelson lived a carefree life, playing with other children in his village. At the age of nine, he was sent to live with his tribe's regent, the leader of the Thembu people. There he watched tribal meetings where everyone who wanted to speak would be heard. It was democracy in its purest form. Community meetings would continue until a consensus was reached. It was not majority rule.

I continue explaining, "Mandela went to college and eventually earned a law degree, but he had very little contact with white people." I read from Mandela's autobiography, *Long Walk to Freedom:* "An African child is born in an Africans Only hospital, taken home in an Africans Only bus, lives in an Africans Only area and attends Africans Only schools, if he attends school at all. When he grows up, he can hold Africans Only jobs, rent a house in Africans Only townships, ride Africans Only trains and be stopped at any time of the day or night and be ordered to produce a pass, without which he can be arrested and thrown in jail" (Mandela, 1994, p. 109).

Mandela decided his life's work was to change the Africans Only policies. He joined the African National Congress, the ANC. In 1941, when Roosevelt and Churchill signed the Atlantic Charter, reaffirming the dignity of each human being, the ANC created its own charter calling for full citizenship for all Africans. I draw a timeline on the chalkboard and continue sharing the history as I show pictures of the South African struggle.

In 1956, Mandela was put on trial for treason and served some prison time. I ask what was happening in the United States during the late 1950s and 1960s. We link the United States' own civil rights movement to this time. Mandela spent years organizing protests within the ANC and helped organize a black army to fight the white government. Meanwhile, the government responded with new laws of greater restriction and violence against black men, women, and children.

By 1962, Mandela was #1 on his country's Most Wanted list. He had been living in hiding for over a year when he was finally captured. His imprisonment was cheered by crowds of white citizens. He was a tremendous threat to the government and was sent to prison on Robbin Island, a small island in the Atlantic Ocean a few miles from Capetown. The ANC continued to launch attacks against the government.

Twenty-eight years later, in 1990, Mandela and other imprisoned leaders were let out of jail. "Do you know anyone who has been in jail for 28 years?" I ask. "Two years later, when black people were allowed to vote for the first time, Mandela became president. He was the first black president of South Africa." I show the pictures of myself in front of Mandela's office and another picture shaking Mandela's hand, or rather the hand of a cardboard Mandela just waiting for tourists.

In the summer of 1996 I had the honor of working for the new Department of Education in South Africa, the first department to have blacks, "coloreds," and whites on staff. I worked with teachers in seven areas of the country, teaching seminars on recent brain research and practical ways of integrating multiple intelligence concepts into their classrooms. The pictures I showed my students linked my life with South Africa, and in turn helped my students feel connected.

My lesson on Mandela is over and I debrief with the children. "What did I do that helped you to listen and learn?" We create a list on the chalkboard: stuff, eye contact, timeline, pictures, personal interest, and personal experiences. "As you plan your presentation, please remember the things that I have just modeled."

ARTS EXPERIENCES AND SYMBOLIC MESSAGES

Our school arts committee makes other curriculum choices that have symbolic meaning. Each year there are many choices in our metropolitan area for student experiences with visual, musical, and dance arts. Our school tends to choose performances that extend our children's understanding of diversity. Students have seen Native American flutist Kevin Locke, the Water Puppets of Vietnam, a Mask Theater production of the story of the Nebraska Rabbi and the Klansman, as well as ethnic dances from around the world.

This week we are preparing for an exhibit on Navajo weaving. The weavings reflect the changes in Navajo life in the 1860s. Scott O'Dell's book, *Sing Down the Moon,* tells the story. During this period, the U.S. government sent Kit Carson to round up the Navahos and walk them to Fort Sumner. The Navahos were held at the fort, living in horrid conditions, for a number of years before being allowed to return to their land. As I read the story aloud, the children experience rich images and emotional connections. Our understanding of the Navajo weavings becomes encased in history.

I am very deliberate as I select literature to read aloud. There simply is not enough time to do everything. I choose stories with themes of intrapersonal development, such as courage, and interpersonal issues between peoples.

RUBY BRIDGES

The story of *Ruby Bridges* is such a book. This beautiful picture book was written by Robert Coles, author of *The Moral Intelligence of Children.* Coles worked with Ruby Bridges in the 1960s when she was the first black child to integrate an elementary school in New Orleans. As I read, we list the characters on the chalkboard, then pose the question, "How would you feel if . . . you were (Ruby, or her mother, father, the teacher, the mob, the federal marshals, etc.)." We review the emotion cards we had used earlier in the year to enrich our vocabulary in relation to each character. Then I ask the children to choose a character and write about possible feelings.

A few days later I connect Ruby's story to the broader context of the civil rights events. I give each student a strip of paper, asking them to fold it in half, then in fourths. I model as I ask them to write "1950" on one end and "1970" on the other. "What's the middle fold going to be?" "1960," they respond. "And what will the other two folds be?" "1955 and 1965," they affirm. "Great! Label them, and I'll explain how Ruby Bridges' story fits into the time of Martin Luther King, Jr."

I share dates one by one, telling the story with an animation fit for these times of fear and ugliness. Again I ask, "How would you feel?"

1954	*Brown v. the Board of Education*
1955	Rosa Parks refuses to give up her seat, Montgomery Bus Boycott
1957	15-year-old Elizabeth Eckford tries to integrate Little Rock, AK—school shut down, lunch counter sit-ins
1960	Ruby Bridges enters elementary school in New Orleans
1961	Freedom riders
1962	James Meredith, first black at the University of Mississippi
1963	Martin Luther King Jr.'s March on Washington D.C., John F. Kennedy assassinated, Civil Rights law passed

Finally, we are ready to view a video on "The Ruby Bridges Story." My students are unusually quiet as they see Ruby's poignant story unfold. The story is so intense that we sit quietly a bit before we begin to discuss the story's implications.

I draw two large interlocking circles, a Venn diagram, on the chalkboard and begin the discussion by asking, "What are the differences between the picture book and the video?" "The principal was in the video. . . . Other Blacks didn't like what Ruby was doing. . . . The marshals drove her to school, in the book she walked. . . . Her mom went to school with her the first number of days. . . ." The points fill the chalkboard, and we ponder the changes.

I turn the focus to feelings. "What words would you use to describe Ruby's feelings?" Feelings of sadness, fear, and pride are shared. We continue discussing other characters, talking about U.S. history, our current lives, fears, and changes.

Understanding the Ruby Bridges story has developed our empathy for other children, for people in differing times and different experiences. It has continued to develop my students' understanding of the nuances of emotional vocabulary. Their writing reinforced language arts skills. The timeline contributed both math skills and social studies content, within the context of dramatic storytelling. Traditional content standards were developed in this process, but on another level symbolic messages were very strong.

Subtle symbolic messages impact children's emotions and motivation. The choices teachers make in our classrooms have the potential to nurture or thwart children's images of themselves, which in turn affect the development of personal intelligence.

5

Reflection, Goals, and Portfolios

"Begin with the end in mind," states Stephen Covey. For my fifth and sixth graders, the end I have in mind is the habit of self-reflection. I want self-reflection to guide their lives, supporting their growth toward positive goals.

As the years have passed, I have become a more deliberate teacher. I realized I'd become a "reflective teacher" before we used the phrase in education. From Sylvia Ashton-Warner and John Dewey, I internalized that I needed to deeply understand each child in my care. I needed to plan for each child's success. Reflection is a key to planning for each child's success.

As teachers, we make hundreds of decisions an hour. Who shall I talk with next? Will I be more successful teaching Tara and Shelly together today, or separately? Why is the energy in our class meeting not well focused today? Shall I try redirecting eye contact, move into a relaxation exercise, or ask Allen to leave the group meeting? Often student teachers have a painful stretch as they begin managing a group of children because they haven't had enough experience to identify all of the factors affecting the classroom climate. Taking time to reflect on the implications of the factors, to internally generate possible actions and chose a path for greatest positive result, is essential. Managing a classroom calls for fast thinking. I enjoy work-

Education is about habits of the mind.
—Ted Sizer in *Smart Schools, Smart Kids,* Edward Fiske (1991), p. 67

I would suggest that self-reflective capacities on the one hand and the ability to recognize what others are thinking and feeling on the other provide the foundation for children to understand, manage, and express the social and emotional aspects of life. Just as children's ability to recognize phonemes is the basic building block of reading letters and words, I believe that being able to recognize their own experience—self-reflective ability—and the ability to recognize others' experiences are the basic building blocks of social and emotional competence.
—Jonathan Cohen (1999), *Educating Minds and Hearts*, p. 11

ing with student teachers, in part, because it forces me to verbalize my own reflective practice.

Each day in our opening routine, we read a quote. Yesterday's reading began, "There's only one corner of the universe you can be certain of improving and that's your own self" (Aldous Huxley). The discussion paragraph begins with, "Most of us are good at telling other people what's wrong with them." I ask, "When have you had someone tell you what's wrong with you?" The children are quick to respond with stories of parents, teachers, and other children telling them what to do. "How did it make you feel?" I continue to probe their experiences. I ask, "Can someone else make you change?" and listen to their explanations.

A bit later it is obvious that Mike is having a particularly hard day. He is jumpy. His face is tense. I inquire, "Mike, you look tense. Did you sleep well last night?"

He grumbles a response, "I don't know."

I need to talk with Mike about his reading test. Mike has the skills of an adult reader but somehow missed half the test. I reflect on a strategy. "Mike, I know you are an excellent reader. I was impressed when I watched you read *Lake Wobegon*. Yet, somehow the reading test results indicated you need a lot of help in reading. I think it's wrong. Do you think you could have messed up on the numbering?" Actually, I think Mike had a bad attitude when he took the test and didn't care about the results. I want him to recognize there are consequences for poor work, but he's not in a good mood today. By using the words, "could have messed up," I give him an out. "Mike, do you want to look at the results now or later?"

"Later."

I leave him for now. I want him to reflect on wasting time doing something poorly the first time and then wasting his time doing it over again. I want to catch students' sloppy habits to help them learn to do their best.

You can't teach what you don't know. I can't teach children to be reflective if I don't practice it myself. On-the-spot, in-the-middle-of-the-action reflection is needed throughout my day.

However, after the children leave each day, my student teacher and I conduct a more thoughtful reflection time. I ask myself, What went well? Which child didn't I spend enough time with today? How do my successes and frustrations today affect what I plan for tomorrow? I make notes on the children's needs and their attitudes while my insights are still fresh. Reflection guides my teaching practice and insures greater success with my students tomorrow.

> *What we typically mean by "consciousness" is self-reflection. . . the mind is able to be aware of its own feelings and desires.*
> —Stanley Greenspan
> (1997), *The Growth of the Mind,* p. 114

STUDENT REFLECTION

On the first day of school I start reflective activities with my students. Modeling with my fingers I ask, "On a scale of one to five, five being fantastic, how did you feel when you got up this morning?" Most of the responses show three or four fingers. "On a scale of one to five, now how do you feel?" Smiles accent students faces as they hold up four and five fingers. I use this scale of one to five for many things throughout the year. "How close are you to being finished with . . . Scale of one to five?"

Self-Evaluation

Name _____ Date _____

The first few days of school have been . . .(horrible) 0—1—2—3—4—5 (very good).

I know the names of . . . (a few) 0—1—2—3—4—5 (all) . . . of the kids in our room.

I have made . . . (a few) 0—1—2—3—4—5 (many) . . . new friends.

I know where to find things in our room. (not at all) 0—1—2—3—4—5 (definitely)

I know how to work on the assignments in our room. (not at all) 0—1—2—3—4—5 (definitely)

I am working "hard enough but not too hard."(not at all) 0—1—2—3—4—5 (definitely)

(Finish the sentence.) I wish . . . _____.

(Finish the sentence.) I would like help on . . . _____.

"How did you feel about the art lesson today, scale of one to five?" "How well did you like . . . Scale of one to five?"

Later that first week I take the pulse of my students with a short written reflection. Their one-half page gives me information about my students but, more important, it encourages self-reflection.

I design many reflective experiences for the children in my care. As students come in from recess, classical music is playing quietly. The children pick up their journals and begin this 15-minute period with a reflection question. When they finish the reflection, they may draw or write as they choose. This process settles my students. Often, as we make the transition into a class meeting, we discuss their responses to the reflection topic.

Typical journal reflections include:

- What three things have you learned lately?
- How have you been nice to someone today?
- What do you think this quote means: "It's not how smart you are, but how you are smart."
- Think of a time you felt teased. Why do you think the other person did it?
- List five things you are good at in math, and five things you want to learn in math.
- As a class we are doing some things well, like walking quietly in the hall. List three other things we are doing well, and three things we could improve.
- Explain the way you study your spelling words so you are successful.
- How does your body feel right now? How does your body feel when you are really focused on learning?
- What do you do to be a friend to someone you've just met?
- Explain why you think we have emotions.

KNOWING WHEN YOU KNOW

Early in the school year, I ask students to reflect on "knowing how they know." After asking some simple yes/no questions, I

Knowing When You Know

Name _____ Date _____

Knowing when you know, and don't know, is an important skill. It requires the reflective skill of self-evaluation. It's an easy thought process for some students and harder for others. Try these questions:

I know how to . . .

tie a knot.	Yes	No
jump rope.	Yes	No
use the school phone.	Yes	No
play kickball.	Yes	No
get on the Internet.	Yes	No
dive off a diving board.	Yes	No
write in cursive.	Yes	No
play Double Dutch.	Yes	No
spell most words I need.	Yes	No
add and subtract negative numbers.	Yes	No

On the back of this half sheet of paper answer these two questions:

1. What does it feel like when you don't know?
2. How do you know when you know something?

ask, "How do you know you know?" This is often a difficult question until we discuss their gut feelings.

I'm not really concerned with the answers for the yes/no questions. The last two are the important ones. I start our meeting with a question, "How do you know when you know?"

"When I know something, it feels easy. I don't need to think of it."

"When I know it, I don't think about it, I just do it."

"When I don't know, I feel confused."

"When I don't know, I feel scared inside."

"My stomach feels icky when I don't know."

This discussion is an important component of building self-awareness, an intrapersonal skill. I encourage my students to listen to the feelings in their bodies. I encourage them to tell an adult when they don't know something. "We need your help to know how to help you," I explain. "We can't get inside your head or your body to know when you know something, or when you need help. We need you to recognize when you don't know and ask a question. Asking questions is a smart thing to do. Sometimes kids think other people will think they are dumb if they ask questions. It's really the opposite. Smart people ask a lot of questions. Smart people don't waste their time not knowing, they ask so they can get things done and learn more." Too often children really don't know that I don't know what they don't know!

END OF THE DAY REFLECTION

On most days, our last 15 minutes together brings another reflection. This is the first year I've ended our days with reflection. A reflection question is written on the chalkboard, the children respond on a 5 × 8 card, and we have a brief conversation.

> Learning will also be smoother if a youngster arrives at school able to reflect on his own behavior, so that, for example, he can tell whether he understands a lesson or assignment and if not, know which part he finds confusing.
> —Stanley Greenspan (1997), The Growth of the Mind, p. 220

- How were you proud of yourself today?
- What did you do today that was kind to someone else?
- When, during our work time, were you really focused? Why?
- What was hard for you today? Why? How can it become better?
- How did you help someone today?
- What are you taking home for homework today?

Here are some responses:

"What I like about myself right now is that I had a really good day."

"I feel tired because I went to sleep late last night."

"Working with my Friendly Helper (a first grader) was enjoyable today."

"I felt like Stressfull because of the work I had to do. But I got a lot of work done. I wasn't bored."

In doing these brief reflections, I encourage students to think about who they are. In time, I hope this reflection becomes a natural habit for my students.

GOAL SETTING

After a child's brain is able to focus, the child can learn to form a plan and act on it. This is the beginning of reflective goal setting. My school uses the framework of Multiple Intelligences for goal setting. These three-way conferences (parents, child, and myself) begin as quickly as I can organize them each school year. I have two goals: to hear from the child, and to establish a positive relationship with the parents. Some children are

Goal Setting:
A Student, Parent, Teacher Process

Student's Name _____ Grade ___ Teacher _____
Fall date _____ Winter date _____ Spring date _____

Intrapersonal:	Self-confidence, responsibility, self-management, ethics . . .
Interpersonal:	Relationship with others, respect, multicultural, solving problems, group work . . .
World Understanding:	Science, social studies, global studies . . .
Linguistic:	Reading, writing, speaking . . .
Logical-Mathematical:	Math, visual, problem solving . . .
Bodily-Kinesthetic:	Physical education, dance, coordination . . .
Visual-Spatial:	Visual arts, geometry, spatial reasoning . . .
Musical:	Vocal, instrumental, cultures . . .
Other goals:	Your life beyond the classroom . . .
Signatures:	Student, parent, teacher . . .

The tie between emotional and physical feeling is thus neither accidental nor symbolic. Indeed, it is wired into our neurology and musculature. Merely acting out the external form of an emotion can produce something of the genuine affect. If you deliberately arrange your features into a happy smile, chances are you'll feel a fleeting ripple of good cheer. If you clench your face into an angry scowl, you'll have a flicker of irritation. Crumpling it into a mask of anguish will call up a slight wave of sorrow. We literally feel our emotions in our bodies, and conversely, our faces and bodies express what we feel.
—Stanley Greenspan (1997), The Growth of the Mind, p. 113

clearly articulate. They have well-developed reflective skills. They explain, "I want to learn about architecture." "I want to improve my computer typing skills." "I want to get better at fractions." These children have thought about who they are and what they want to learn. Setting goals seem like natural steps for these children.

The goal-setting process is difficult for other children. I start the conversation, "Shelly, have you thought about your goals this year?" She shrugs her shoulders. "What are you interested in?"

"I like to make things, and I like to dance," she replies. I've noticed Shelly's strengths in kinesthetic activities.

"Would you like a goal of making some things instead of a written book report?" She nods. "Would you be willing to do a dance to describe a feeling?" She shakes her head, no.

I move on and become more directive, "In the Intrapersonal skills, are you good at getting assignments done on time? Should that be a goal?" She nods, and I write it on our form. Some children have many goals. With children like Shelly, we'll only set a few goals. She needs to keep a specific focus. "Shelly, what about asking questions when you're stuck. Asking questions is a smart thing to do. Could you have a goal of asking more questions?" She OKs that idea.

In time, I invite mom and dad to share their goals for Shelly. Their major concern is improving her reading skills. Yes, I'll work hard to help Shelly with her comprehension, but my heart remembers so many kinesthetic children who find sitting still in order to read very difficult. I will try to help Shelly make personal connections with what she is reading. Maybe she'll learn to dramatize, to put what she's read into her kinesthetic body.

The student who doesn't ask doesn't learn.
—The Talmudic sages

A goal for Matt is to smile more. Joseph has a goal to sit up in meetings, instead of slouching, so he looks "as if" he is paying attention. Both of these goals are aimed at practicing behaviors that can change internal attitudes. A frown or a slouchy posture sends a message. I hope these boys will learn to reorganize their body messages.

ANDY'S GOALS

Andy's mother failed to show for our conference once again. I've made numerous calls to her about scheduling a goal-setting conference. I've sent home notes. Twice she promised to come in the evening and didn't show up. I sent a letter on school stationery suggesting I'd drive Andy home at the end of the school day, pick her up, and we could all go to a coffee shop for treats. No response.

Andy's mother finally comes to school because of behavior problems. I am glad to meet her, but I had hoped to establish a trusting relationship before dealing with discipline issues. We talk about the behaviors that created the problem for Andy. Then I try to accomplish the goal-setting process. Essentially Andy's mother declares the goals:

- Get your work done on time
- Have a good attitude
- Do what the adults tell you
- Ask for help when you're stuck
- Get to bed on time

I write the list, noting in my body how different this feels. These goals are orders from on high. They do not represent Andy being thoughtfully involved in his own life. My sense is that Andy's mother doesn't use reflective thought patterns, but models the reflexive behaviors that Andy uses so often. But, this conference is a start; I have something to work with, though not satisfactory by any means.

Andy doesn't even have the beginnings of a "crystal clear image" of what to do to meet the goals listed on his conference form. In contrast, Jim's goals are very clear to him: "I want to learn negative

> To accomplish any goal, you must have a crystal clear image of that goal and keep it uppermost in your mind. We know that by maintaining that image, the "how-to" steps necessary for the realization of that goal will begin to emerge spontaneously. If you cannot image the goal, the "how-to" steps will never emerge, and you'll never do it. Clearly the first step to any achievement is to dare to imagine that you can do it.
>
> —Marilyn King (a two-time Olympic pentathlete; 1988), "Ordinary Olympians," *In Context*, p. 14

numbers and unknowns in pre-algebra." There is a world of difference between these two sixth-grade boys.

Goals must become a living process if the children are going to have a clear image of what they are trying to accomplish. One way I bring clarity is by asking each student to imagine and paint a large colored picture of achieving one of his or her goals. As these pictures are shared with the class I ask, "How does it feel to have accomplished this goal? Who is proud of you?" This quality attention reinforces the goal and the importance of working hard for it. Another day, I ask students to rate their progress toward a goal on a scale of zero (haven't started yet) to five (accomplished with pride). We conference with parents again in February. We share portfolios and progress toward goals with parents during "Achievement Days" in December and May.

HOMEWORK

For many fifth and sixth graders, doing more homework is a needed developmental step. Self-awareness and self-management responsibilities increase at this age. On Monday mornings we discuss the assignments for the week. Students use individual calendars to write assignment due dates. Some children psychologically gulp and then manage this increased responsibility. These children learned the intrapersonal skill of self-management and have the motivation to be successful in school. Somewhere along the way, they have had nourishing support to make this stretch without a crisis.

Other children can't seem to remember assignments, even though they are clearly written on the chalkboard and discussed daily. These children tend to be more distractible and are not able to attend well. They may not have learned to trust that adults will help them if they ask for help. They may be living in the eternal present, not having developed an internal sense of time. Regardless, these children need more coaching to master their new responsibilities. They need tools to understand what they are expected to do, and tools to support their self-awareness of whether their work is done. These are tools of reflection and self-evaluation.

Allen needs a daily reminder: "Allen, what do you need to remember to take home today?" We planned that he was not to leave for his bus until he reviewed his homework. "Is there something you need to get before you leave, Allen?" Allen is a kinesthetic and visual learner, so I encourage him to utilize those strategies. "Allen, where are you going to do your homework? Will you be comfortable so your body can focus? Picture yourself doing your homework, do you have what you need? Can you feel how great it will be to be done? What does your body want to do for a reward?" It took a long time, but eventually Allen learned the habit of reflecting on his responsibilities before leaving school.

Next to no consideration has been paid to the fundamental necessity—leading the child to realize a problem as his own, so that he is self-induced to attend in order to find out its answer.
—John Dewey (1990), *The School and Society: The Child and the Curriculum*, p. 149

My role is not to punish Allen for forgetting his homework. It's not my duty to nag him. It is my role to try strategies that lead to the internalization of his responsibilities. By age seven, many children have mastered internal self-talk, which guides the direction of their actions. This internal talk connects current actions to what happens next. There is a sense of control in understanding cause and effect. There is a sense that "I am what I am today because of the choices I made yesterday." Allen hasn't made this internal connection yet.

HALLOWEEN SCARY STORIES

October is a great time to have students really invest themselves in a three-draft story, a scary story. I ask students about their characters and their plots. In order for them to be able to make significant revisions, we make sure all first drafts are typed on the children's individual computer disks. Word processing is necessary for this three-draft story. I show students copies of the chapter I am writing, modeling the extensive corrections that are made with each draft.

After the first draft is done, we have another class discussion about good writing. Before the children started writing, we generated a list of criteria for a good story.

I ask the children to recall what they listed and we regenerate it on the chalkboard. "OK, this is what we think makes a

What Makes a Good Story

Beginning, middle, and end	0—1—2—3—4—5
Supporting details	0—1—2—3—4—5
Good plot	0—1—2—3—4—5
Punctuation correct	0—1—2—3—4—5
Spelling correct	0—1—2—3—4—5

good story. This week you need to find a friend to help you edit your story. My friend, Renee, helps edit my writing. You will edit your friend's story. This is what needs to be done." I point to the chalkboard. "Watch for periods and capital letters. Make note of words that come out of someone's mouth, these should be in quotes. If you're not sure, ask your partner if the words were spoken. Watch for changes that indicate there should be a paragraph. Underline any words you think might be misspelled. Discuss the characters. Are they described well enough? Do you suggest more description? Is there a clear beginning, middle, and end for the story? You are your partner's helper. Work with your partner to improve each other's writing."

"After your partner helps you think about your writing, you need to get your disk and make improvements. Finally, turn in your planning sheet, your first draft, and your second draft."

I encourage another kind of student reflection as I read the second drafts. Using an erasable pencil, I put a check on the line if the child needs to check for a spelling error, and a dot to indicate there is a punctuation error. I write little on a child's work; she has invested a lot of herself in the story. If I feel the need to make comments, I use a Post-it note. The point is to nudge her reflection and encourage her proofreading skills. I conference briefly with each child. "On this line there's a check. Can you check for a spelling error? The dot means there is a punctuation error. Can you find it?" This is very different than using traditional editing marks and simply showing the child each and every mistake.

Some children have trouble developing a clear story line. Others need work on paragraphs. Typically, most fifth and sixth graders need work on the punctuation of conversation. Our students head back to the computers for additional corrections.

It is the day before Halloween, and the final copies of the scary stories are ready to be shared. We divide into three circles and hand out the original list of criteria that will be their evaluation form. Stories are passed to the left two times, read quietly, and given an evaluation by a peer reader. Then they are passed again, until three or four students read each work. Evaluations and stories are returned to the writer and the children informally discuss each other's work. "I really thought your story was great. It was so spooky right until the end." Students have had the opportunity to share their work with both adults and peers. They have gotten feedback from four or more people. Now it's time for a final self-reflection before the stories are laid to rest in their portfolios.

> Teachers will not have a major impact on the way kids use their minds until they come to know how their students' mind work. Teachers cannot help young people make sense of things if they do not know what is not sensible to them, if they do not have the time to answer their questions. They cannot improve a student's writing if there isn't time to read it, reflect on it, and then meet occasionally with the student about his or her work.
> —Deborah Meier in *Schools That Work,* George Wood

Children must develop the skills of directing their attention, their focus, on relevant information. Children who had trouble attending to the criteria for good stories had lower evaluations. To learn, you must be able to attend and process

---

Three-Draft Scary Story

Name_____ Date _____

What was your title? _____

1. Do you have your planning sheet? _____ Your first draft? _____
   Your second draft? _____ Your final copy? _____ Why? _____
2. What did you improve from your first draft to your final copy?

   _____

3. What did you learn about writing? _____

   _____

4. How could you improve your story even more? _____

   _____

information. Processing means playing around with the information within your mind. The skill of self-reflection is crucial for this mental "playing around" of information processing. Children who feel threatened have greater difficulty hearing feedback and processing information. For some children this was the first time their peers had given them feedback. Peer feedback is a powerful form of reflection.

The scary story assignment wasn't simply about writing skills. It was also about building skills of reflection on their own work and the work of others. It was an experience in dealing with feelings of embarrassment and pride, of investing oneself by using one's strengths, and of asking for help.

PORTFOLIOS

In September we began the process. We collected all checked-in papers and had an afternoon "portfolio sort." In this first sorting, I asked students to classify their papers into groups. Then they organized each section according to dates and made some evaluative comments. This reflection process was difficult for many students.

After the first portfolio reflection, I conferenced with the children to further coach their thinking. Some were able to think about their work without much help from me. Many, too many, showed lack of depth. Answers like, "I don't know," led me to believe I needed to spend even more time helping my students learn to reflect. So, in conferences with each child, I encouraged greater depth of thought. For some students, I literally needed to lead his or her thinking to evoke thoughtful comments. Portfolio reflection was not a natural process at this time.

It's November and the children's portfolios are bulging. We have saved every paper of each child's work. In previous years, I saved some papers and sent others home periodically. But, at a Harvard workshop, a wise leader commented on the symbolic meaning of throwing anything away. Besides the value of clear documentation, there is an emotional message. When a child has put any amount of work into producing something, even minimal, it is respectful to value the work by saving it. Thus,

Portfolio Reflection

Name _____Date _____

When you do a step in this process, X it off.

_____1. Sort your portfolio into categories. Use a colored-paper page as a divider for each section. The sections are like chapters in a book.

_____2. Check to see that each paper, in each section, has a date on it. Put the materials in dated order. The first papers are dated early September, the last papers are the most recent.

_____3. Write three, or more, statements about **each section** on the colored page divider. *For example: The science section has papers related to the monarch butterflies.*

"I didn't know _____ when we started in _____ (date)."

"I learned _____."

For example in math: "My papers show that I've done a lot of work on
_____."

"In September, _____ was hard enough, but now it is easy."

For example on reflection, end-of-the-day papers: "My record of what I'm reading is _____." "I use full sentences when I write my daily reflection rather than just a word or two."

_____4. Decide which math papers are the most important to keep in your portfolio to show your work. Which papers could you give to your parents to show them the quality of your work? Clip the papers for your parents together with a paper clip. Use a sheet of colored paper and write your parents a note telling them about your math work.

_____5. What have you learned about yourself by thinking about what you have done?

_____

_____

_____6. We always can improve the quality of our work. Make a two-part plan on how you will improve:

"I will _____."

"I will _____."

Portfolio Reflection

Name _____ Date _____

The purpose of portfolios, the collection of your work, is to be able to better understand who you are and how well you are learning. Reflection is a difficult skill, but a very important one. It is important for you to develop the skills of thinking about what you are doing. Look at each section to fill this out.

In my **math section** I have _____ different pieces of work. I have worked on these concepts: _____
_____.

On a rating of 1 to 5, I feel I have been "working hard enough but not too hard."

_____

My **science section** shows my work on

_____

_____

On a scale of 1 to 5, I feel my work has been careful and clear. _____
I have enjoyed _____
My **writing section** shows how I have improved on _____

_____

Draw an arrow to the column that applies to you in each of these writing skills:

I need to work more on this   **I feel I do this well**

Getting ideas to write about
Brainstorming and webbing my idea
Using capital letters and punctuation
Writing in paragraphs
Using commas
Writing conversation
Editing and improving my first draft

My **art section** has _____ pieces. Art is _____ for me.
I do _____ well. I could improve on _____.

Portfolio Reflection *(continued)*

My **miscellaneous section** has information on my learning style. I think I learn best by using (circle one) auditory—visual—kinesthetic strategies. My natural way I approach the world is (circle one)

Extraversion—Introversion—pretty balanced. The thing I like the best in this section is _____.

This year is going well for me.   (not at all) 0—1—2—3—4—5 (great)

I ask for help right away when I don't
    understand something.   0—1—2—3—4—5

I turn my work in on time.   0—1—2—3—4—5

I am comfortable sharing my ideas with
    my classmates.   0—1—2—3—4—5

I have improved the most on _____.

I would like to improve on _____.

each child has a pile. Now we need to make meaning of the piles.

It's February. We sort portfolios again. Now children have a mass of work to consider. There is the three-draft scary story, many math experiences, more science, and significant art-work.

The February portfolio reflection goes smoother. Children have the concept of sorting and organizing. We have collected a lot of materials. They enjoy looking at what they accomplished. I ask them to select a "My Best Work" piece out of each of their portfolio sections for individual "Best Work" posterboards. With the child's name in the center, I design 3 × 4 posterboards honoring the selected items from their portfolios. The "Best Work" posters fill our room and flow into the hall. It feels good to see the variety of selections these children have made.

REFLECTION AND SELF-TALK

Most learning activities provide an opportunity for reflective thinking, if teachers choose to include that component. Some afternoons we play the commercially available "24" game in cooperative groups. Students enjoy the competition with supportive groups of three children. Children who have not developed internal self-talk, however, tend to get frustrated. The game provides four numbers that, using any mathematical process you can think of, result in the answer "24." Often there are multiple ways to get the answer. We play in teams so there is cooperation within the competition.

Teams get points for correct answers but it is random, through the drawing of TEAM cards, so team scores tend to be quite even. Each student can be successful if he is engaged. I teach the strategy of completing a series of operations with the numbers, using calculators, and recording the process. "Then," I instruct, "reflect on whether you should try to make your answer turn out larger or smaller. Think about what happened."

Children who have developed internal self-talk easily think of another sequence and give it a try. Other children don't seem to have a clue. I explain again, "Write down what you are thinking and then use the calculator to figure out the answer. Keep a record. Decide what you want to do and try something else." It feels as if the children who are frustrated aren't talking to themselves. The absence of internal self-talk is the cause of their difficulties.

TEAM cards are simple to make and provide a way to organize students for many purposes. I use 3×5 index cards and the eight colors in a marker box. I write one letter from the word TEAM on each card, creating a set of four cards in a color. This gives me eight sets of TEAM cards. When I want cooperative group roles I use the letters as a designated job—T is the task manager, E is the encourager, A is the articulator who writes and reports back, and M is the mover who gets supplies. Sometimes I randomly hand out the cards and have the vowels of one color and the consonants of that same color work together as pairs. For the "24" game I want three children together and don't need a mover, so I take out the M cards.

Jane Healy (1998), in *Failure to Connect,* voices concern about too much screen time, whether TV or computers, and a lack of inner speech. There are indications that screen time for children under age eight blocks the normal development of language. Are the changing patterns of children's lives affecting their inner speech?

The developmental timetable for inner speech is from four to six years of age. If self-talk is missing, the child has no voice to carry out reflection, no guide in deciding what to do next. Tara, a fifth grader, seems to have no internal self-talk. I model the thought process: "Tara, how are you going to get to 24?"

"I donno," she replies passively.

"This is how I would try it. First, I decide which number to start with. I have to use all four numbers 3, 6, 6, and 8. I choose 6. Now do I want to multiply or add? I'll multiply the 6. That's 36. That's too big. Now what shall I do? How about if I subtract the 8. That's 28, but I have another 6 to use. Tara, do we need to get a bigger or a smaller answer?" Math thinking is based on the habits of thinking. You must decide what to pay attention to, make a plan, do it, and reflect on what happened. These intrapersonal self-management habits must be developed. If self-talk hasn't developed as a natural process, we teachers need to work very deliberately toward modeling inner speech.

David Elkind suggests, to have a successful school beginning, children need to be able to listen, express themselves, follow directions, bring a task to completion, and cooperate with others. If a child hasn't learned to focus her attention, to stay emotionally calm, and to hear an inner voice, Elkind predicts she will not be successful. Emotions direct our attention and attention drives our intentions.

Good readers use inner dialogues and imagery to make sense of words. They are involved with the text. I teach students to first skim the material to pick up a general sense of the topic, then to look at the questions to know what they're supposed to be understanding. Finally, I encourage them to ask their own questions about the topic. "Why is this important?" "What is the author trying to explain?" To be a good reader you have to comprehend the words, then link them to other ideas you understand. This process requires inner self-talk. Development of an inner voice is key for reflective thought.

"Pay attention," we tell children. Recent insights on child development explain how complex it is to pay attention. After the age of seven, children should have developed the ability to screen out certain stimuli and select the important auditory and visual stimuli. But who defines "important stimuli? For one child in my class, the important stimuli seems to be entertaining other children, rather than focusing on what I am trying to teach. Defining important stimuli is an emotional decision: "What will give me what I want?"

PORTFOLIOS AGAIN

The year is coming to a close. I wander through the portfolios of my students—the large graphs, paintings, timelines, best papers, reports, and photographs. How, I ask myself, can I improve on the children's final presentation of their portfolios to their parents? In the past, I have helped students present well organized portfolios with a significant reflection piece. I have coached them on how to explain things to their parents, but . . . I reflect. The insight sought comes with an image. We will bind the final portfolio selections with large plastic combs like we use to bind reports!

The final portfolio process begins. Children select key items from each section of their massive array of work. They use Post-it notes to explain why they chose the piece. They choose some pieces to show their work at the beginning of the year, and other pieces to show their best work. Children type an introduction consisting of what went really well this year and what were their personal struggles. They write a reflective three-page paper summarizing their experiences during this school year. They organize their papers and create a table of contents. They decorate the section dividers of assembled papers and all is ready for binding.

Children also select items for their longitudinal portfolio, the portfolio containing items from each year they have been in our school. This portfolio is given to their parents the night of

> *Reflecting is fundamental—the capacity to assume distance on oneself and one's experiences proves the sine qua non of effective accomplishment. That reflection typically proceeds in two directions: first, toward an examination of one's own strengths and liabilities; second, toward an examination of the lessons from daily experiences.*
> —Howard Gardner (1997), *Extraordinary Minds*, p. 152

eighth-grade graduation. There is significant discussion whether an item belongs in this year's portfolio or whether it should go into the longitudinal portfolio.

Parents are delighted with the finished portfolios. These bound portfolios are keepsakes, not just an exhibition of their children's learning. Parents thank me again and again for the portfolios: their child's work but my initiative. They are thrilled.

Teaching intrapersonal reflection skills and goal setting can be difficult. It is significantly more complicated than teaching multiplication. Often I wonder if my strategies are making a difference, then one day I realize that Tara is really thinking about what she's doing, and Allen has improved on his goal of getting work done. These children are making progress, inch by inch, toward a stronger foundation of self-awareness, reflection, and goal setting, which will serve them as productive intrapersonal habits.

The main advantage of portfolios for students is that students learn to take responsibility for collecting evidence about their own work and assessing their own progress. They become more actively involved in applying criteria of learning and motivation and understand the standards of performance that are expected of them. They become engaged in self-assessment, which is the critical internalization of both parents' and teachers' standards and expectations.
—Nadine Lambert and Barbara McCombs (1998), *How Students Learn*, p. 204

6

Children in My Life

My school covers a half city block in Minneapolis. We have a range of socioeconomic families, from very poor to well off. We have families created by adoption. We have single-parent families, and families with two moms or two dads.

My class of 25 fifth and sixth graders consists of 11 girls and 14 boys. Sixteen are students of color. We have recent arrivals and children of poverty. Halimo recently celebrated the one-year anniversary of her arrival in the United States. She had spent the last six years in an Ethiopian refugee camp. Panta's parents immigrated from Laos after the Vietnam War. Stacey lives in a large Native American housing complex in our city.

Kaelyn was out of school for three weeks, traveling with her family to visit friends and relatives in France and Cyprus. We e-mailed her greetings and she quickly returned messages to every classmate, which we read aloud. The children without e-mail experience were in shock. How could Kaelyn connect with us from across the world?

Matt, Jerod, and Tim competed in the weeklong national chess tournament in Phoenix. They did very well.

Our children's cognitive ability scores, an indication of IQ in the old sense, range from 65 to 145. This year, one child was beaten to the extent that child-protection workers documented the incident with photographs. One child's parents essentially did all of her work, developing their brains, but leaving her feeling even less capable of doing her own work. The children in my classroom are experiencing very different lives.

Four of our boys are on medications for Attention Deficit Disorder (ADD). I sense the parents of each child carry a heavy burden in making the decision to use drugs. Deeply loving their sons, seeing their sons with significant problems, knowing that there is a potential genetic link, feeling a responsibility to ensure their child's success—each parent carries ever-present concern in his or her heart. Medication is not an easy decision. I ponder the increasing literature on ADD and ADHD (Attention Deficit Hyperactivity Disorder). I've read Russell Barkley's, Thom Hartmann's, and Thomas Armstrong's explanations. I've studied Daniel Amen's SPECT images of ADD brains compared to others. We are learning more, but the range of differences in children is still perplexing.

> For some time, researchers have been examining provocative links between brain functioning and the positive effects of physical activity. Regular exercise increases the blood supply to the brain, thus giving it a greater oxygen and energy supply—for better mental abilities. In addition, chemicals secreted by the brain during and after exercise enable it to deal better with stress and anxiety, counteract the effects of depression, and help children learn more efficiently by harnessing the positive power of emotions for learning and memory. Scientists also suggest that the type of exercise most likely to achieve these positive effects is "unforced," the type of spontaneous play in which children just naturally engage.
> —Jan Healy (1998), *Failure to Connect*, p. 121

When I began teaching in the mid-1960s, these labels had not been invented. What is causing the difference in children's lives? Some reports believe there is a link in our children to the changes in our lifestyles, specifically TV, computer games, food issues, lack of physical activities, and unsafe neighborhoods that limit the opportunities to just play.

MATT—BRIGHT AND HAS ADD

Matt is a bright computer expert. In the past number of years, his school life has been extremely stressful. In his reaction to the stresses, he became silly and compulsive. As his inappropriate social interactions increased, his relationships with peers deteriorated. Last year was a stressful year. There was an uncomfortable energy-tension surrounding him as he transferred into our classroom early in the spring. In the beginning of our relationship, I needed to be continually aware of what Matt was doing and with whom so that I could sense an escalation of tension in his body and voice. I would gently intervene and redirect him to a more productive activity, removing him from a potential self-damaging engagement.

Before school this August, Matt's mom, Kathy, called. "Should I home-school him?" she asked. "Then he wouldn't get into the negative interactions with other kids." Last spring I had given Matt the entrance test for our middle school algebra class. He had gotten a perfect score. Kathy and I talked. I felt Matt needed to develop his strength in math by taking the algebra class. Although his peer interactions had been painful, Matt needed to be around kids his own age to improve his social skills. We compromised. Often kids with ADD have trouble sleeping, and our 7:45 morning start time was a constant source of difficulty for Matt. Matt would sleep a bit later and come in time for the algebra class. He'd join us for a few hours of school community time. Private tutoring and home schoolwork would focus on his writing skills. Although Matt's math thinking is excellent, he has significant difficulty writing. This

Dr. Amen, a clinical neuroscientist and child and adolescent psychiatrist from California, believes ADD is related to the underactive activity of the basal ganglia, toward the center of the brain. This area is involved with the integration of feelings, thoughts, and movement.

He writes, "Shifting and smoothing fine motor behavior is another basal ganglia function and is essential to handwriting and motor coordination. Again, let's use the example of attention deficit disorder. Many children and adults with ADD have very poor handwriting. The act of handwriting is difficult and often stressful for them. Their writing may be choppy or sloppy. In fact, many teens and adults with ADD print instead of writing in cursive. They find printing easier because it is not a smooth, continuous motor movement, but rather a start-and-stop motor activity. Many people with ADD also complain that they have trouble getting their thoughts out of their head and onto paper, a term called finger agnosia (the fingers cannot tell what the brain is thinking)" (Amen, 1998, p. 84).

spring Matt qualified for special education services in writing. The point was to agree on a flexible plan for Matt's greatest success.

One day this winter, Matt was extremely frustrated about a decision I had made. He was monopolizing my time. Finally I said, "Matt, you don't have to like it but it's my decision. Breathe deeply, relax, and look at me." He did it! He stopped the incessant complaining and breathed deeply. He visibly relaxed. "OK," he said, "but I don't like it." WOW! I thought, he's really maturing. All the hard times are worth it!

Today, Matt usually smiles. The cloud of tension has dissipated. He is well liked in our classroom. He is approachable. He is always ready to help with a computer glitch. His mom recently commented, "Matt feels safe here." I smile with satisfaction. This child's potential is blossoming. He is on the right track now. I give thanks.

The interplay of intrapersonal and interpersonal intelligences is often indistinguishable. Matt's slowly increasing ability to manage himself allowed him to have better relationships with other children. Although we coached him on how to connect with other children, how to relate to his audience, he had to learn to manage his impulses to do so. Good interpersonal skills are dependent on intrapersonal skills.

KAELYN—BRIGHT AND INSECURE

Kaelyn bursts into tears and leaves the room. Our student teacher follows her. Kaelyn is a young fifth grader. She still embodies an innocent spirit. She is an excellent reader and has high expectations for herself. In this case, as a number of times in these first few weeks of school, she didn't understand the concept I was teaching to the group. She panicked. Tears flooded her eyes and she escaped to the hallway.

A bit later I talk with her, "Kaelyn, I know you are really smart. Do you know you are smart?"

She nods her head.

"I also know you get really upset when you don't understand what's happening. Right?" Agreed. "We need to make a plan so you can breathe deeply when you start to get afraid. Can you breathe deeply with me now?" We breathe together for

Schools play an essential role in preparing our children to become knowledgeable, responsible, caring adults.

Knowledgeable. Responsible. Caring. Behind each word lies an educational challenge. For children to become knowledgeable, they must be ready and motivated to learn, and capable of integrating new information into their lives. For children to become responsible, they must be able to understand risks and opportunities, and be motivated to choose actions and behaviors that serve not only their own interests but those of others. For children to become caring, they must be able to see beyond themselves and appreciate the concerns of others; they must believe that to care is to be part of a community that is welcoming, nurturing, and concerned about them.

—Maurice Elias et al. (1997), *Promoting Social and Emotional Learning,* p. 1

a few moments. "Now, when you breathe out I want you to say, 'the teachers will help me, the teachers will help me.' Let's try it together." We breathe and quietly repeat the phrase, "The teachers will help me, the teachers will help me." "Kaelyn, it's smart to ask questions. I want you to ask questions. Can we make a plan? When you don't understand something, I'd like you to breathe deeply and try to calm yourself. Can you think well when you get upset? Remember our talk about the brain? Breathe deeply, calm yourself, remember the teachers will help you, then ask a teacher as soon as you're able to. We will help you. You need to help yourself notice you're getting nervous, and breathe to calm yourself."

Kaelyn is making a transition from the time her excellent reading could carry her through tasks successfully to the more complex tasks in fifth grade. She is working to develop basic intrapersonal self-management skills, that is, to be able to notice an increasing body tension, to calm herself, and refocus her attention.

TIM—BRIGHT AND SENSITIVE

Tim is another very bright and emotionally sensitive fifth grader. Tears come quickly for Tim. As we are goal setting, we discuss the importance of identifying feelings before they swell up into tears. As the year progressed, Tim consciously worked on understanding the subtle signs of emotion in his body. Tim's quiet soul was always ready to help another student. I observed as Tim's relationship with different children strengthened. It was amazing to watch a very streetwise boy gradually seek out Tim's help and develop a valued friendship.

Tim was always ready to work in any assigned cooperative group. Although he became frustrated with other children's lower standards of work, Tim's leadership continued to help solve problems.

I smiled with gratefulness as I watched Tim curl up against his mom and read one afternoon, so unaffected by the pressures of the world today. He was still enjoying the safety of his mom's snuggling.

Tim easily qualified to take the algebra class with the seventh and eighth graders, but we jointly decided the algebra wasn't as important as the stability of one teacher in a personally nurturing environment.

TARA—STRUGGLING WITH LEARNED HELPLESSNESS

Tara is also a fifth grader. I am shocked at her low skill levels. Her previous teacher tells me she has better skills than she's showing—she just doesn't like to do her work. Tara hasn't decided that learning is something she needs to do for herself. Schoolwork is framed as something the teacher makes you do, rather than something for her growth. Repeatedly I have sat with her, teaching her to use the ones/tens blocks to regroup in subtraction. Today, I teach the process once again. I think she's got the idea and move on to help another child. Tara pushes the blocks aside and starts working a problem with just her pencil. She's confused again. I return to encourage her to use the blocks, and set up the next equation. She rocks in her chair and quits entirely.

I am teaching perimeter, area, and volume with a collection of small boxes. "Perimeter is like a fence. It goes around the edge of an area." I run my finger across the edge of the box and demonstrate how to measure the four sides in centimeters. I ask children to measure their boxes. Many are easily successful. Tara doesn't try. "Tara," using her box, "measure the four sides like this." I demonstrate without giving the numbers. She doesn't touch the box.

The better we know our children individually, the more we know about them culturally, and the deeper we understand the patterns of their development, the better able we are to make appropriate and meaningful changes to the institutions and practices of education.
—Chip Wood (1999),
Time to Teach, Time to Learn, p. 35

I continue with the other children. "Area is like a rug. Take a piece of graph paper. Measure the size of a square on the graph paper. Yes,

If students won't let a teacher know what level they are on—by asking a question or revealing their ignorance—they will not learn or grow. People cannot pretend for long; eventually they will be found out. Often an admission of ignorance is the first step in our education.
—Stephen Covey (1991), *Principle-Centered Leadership,* p. 80

the squares are centimeters, so you label your answer as centimeter square. Now put your box on top of the graph paper and trace around it. Then cut it out and fit your 'rug' inside your box." Hands are active; but not Tara's. She won't try.

Questions about perimeter and area have been clarified. I take out the centimeter cubes and, after a similar discussion about volume, children start filling their boxes. Tara is sulking, looking off into space. She could have learned this. It was developmentally appropriate, but somehow it was not emotionally safe to try.

I gather further information from adults who have known this family. Apparently the older children have a similar pattern. There is a silence that runs through their lives, a silence penetrating their interaction with the outer world. How do I unlock the key to real communication with this child?

Late in the year Tara has begun to interact more often with me. She prefers to learn from other students, especially Kate. She still does no homework and "freezes up" when expected to learn something new. This strategy is documented in abused children. The dissociative response of "freezing" is linked to emotional maltreatment. It seems, for Tara, this strategy has become established as the norm, a "fight or flight" response that shuts down in self-defense.

JACOB—IN CRISIS

Jacob, a sixth grader, embodies all the complexities of emotional hijacking. His difficulties, which require adult intervention, are daily. It's only the middle of October, but today marked the seventh time he has needed to leave school in the middle of the day due to behavior difficulties. Many of his personal behaviors are inappropriate, but his rage is my greatest concern. He becomes angry because "they" are "always" doing whatever has triggered the latest outburst. He is unable to label his feelings with words. He is unable to connect his own behavior with cause-and-effect thinking. He is emotionally stuck in the stage of a two- to four-year-old. Somehow, along the way,

Jacob did not get the practice and feedback needed to develop basic emotional skills. Now, instead of being able to use words and thoughts to reflect on a dislike, he reflexively lashes out. There seems to be no well-used pathway to the frontal lobes to reflect on his past experiences. He reacts with all the fear his amygdala can muster. Other children are understandably afraid of him. His tall, overweight body, matched with his out-of-control behaviors, is enough to intimidate most people. He is a very bright young man in terms of traditional intellect, but can't function socially well enough to remain in his advanced classes during a week. His best friend in the room is an intellectually limited fifth-grade boy who can hardly read. This friend sticks with Jacob.

> Because physical flight often is not possible for very young children, they freeze when they have no control over threatening events. The freezing response allows a child time to process and evaluate the stressor. Some caretakers, however, often interpret a freezing response as noncompliance to their instructions, which, if frustration arises, may open the door to further mistreatment. The brain's organization may be further altered if the additional maltreatment lasts long enough. Eventually, youngsters feel anxious and frustrated all the time, even when experiences are nonthreatening.
> —Barbara Lowenthal (1999), "Effects of Maltreatment and Ways to Promote Children's Resiliency," *Childhood Education*, p. 205

Of course, I don't give up on helping Jacob modify his behavior, but it's important to understand the difficulty of changing his behaviors. Apparently, he missed the "window of opportunity" to move through this toddler stage of emotional development. If a brain doesn't hear language during the critical window of opportunity, it is significantly more difficult later to learn language. Similarly, Jacob, a bright 12-year-old, is stuck in the behavior of a 3-year-old's emotions.

Our brains have a set point for body temperature. Any fluctuation is brought to the system's attention and corrective measures are begun by the brain stem. Likewise there are set points for the amount of serotonin and noradrenaline in our brains. Serotonin is a calming neurotransmitter. A low level of serotonin has been linked to violent behavior. Noradrenaline is the opposing neurotransmitter. Its purpose is to alert the body to danger. High levels of noradrenaline are linked to impulsive behaviors. Regardless of the cause of the imbalance, there is a chemistry related to rageful behavior. Changing the angry outbursts of

> A child who doesn't have this ability to identify angry feelings and create an idea of them in her mind—that is, label the feelings and then express those angry or competitive feelings in play or through words—is going to have difficulty interacting with other children who have that ability.
> —Stanley Greenspan (1993), *Playground Politics*, p. 34

this 12-year-old is more complicated because his anger set points seem habituated differently from "normal" behaviors.

Impulsive behaviors are commonly linked with low levels of serotonin. Impulsive children have difficulty waiting their turn in reciprocal behavior, a needed social skill. In the classroom, behaviors related to "taking turns" include normal conversations between children, class discussions, and impatience when the teacher can't pay attention this exact minute. Impatience in taking turns creates tension throughout the day.

The combination of low serotonin and high noradrenaline is linked with impulsive aggression toward others, and I certainly have seen Jacob's rage directed at others. When both chemicals are low, aggression is aimed at oneself. Jacob has banged his head against the door frame in a repetitive motion. He has gagged himself. He has placed both thumbs against the front of his neck and proceeded to choke himself. He has put a plastic garbage bag over his head. This is a very unhappy young man. I fear for his life and for those who are on the receiving end of his rage.

Many people inherit a gene that makes them more susceptible to low serotonin. But early life experiences—living in a violent household or a normal one—appear to determine how that gene will be expressed; that is, whether serotonin levels will be set on low, normal, or high. Low levels seem to be an adaptation to a threatening environment. Low serotonin allows an individual to be more impulsive.
—Ronald Kotulak (1996),
Inside the Brain, p. 69

I have no direct knowledge of Jacob's earlier life. I do know his father is extremely controlling. During our goal-setting conference, Jacob's father consistently cut him off, with "Shut up." Another time his father intimated a threat that Jacob had better behave at school or he would *make* him behave! Dr. Bruce Perry, who examined the children released from the Branch Davidian compound in Waco (during a standoff with federal agents), explains, "It is adaptive to be impulsive in that (abusive) setting. If you wait, very frequently you will be victimized. So it's highly adaptive to be hypervigilant, to be overly reactive and impulsive, to actually act before you're acted upon" (Kotulak, 1996, p. 70).

Although it's helpful for me to understand there is brain chemistry involved in Jacob's behavior, it doesn't solve the problem of how to help him change his behaviors. In fact, it makes me more aware of the depth of the issues in this troubled young man.

Quickly recognizing anger can be an important survival skill for such children. But while spotting anger might help a child avoid a beating, it also can cause problems outside the home.

The research of Seth Pollak, assistant professor of psychology and psychiatry at the University of Wisconsin-Madison, showed computerized pictures of happy, fearful, and angry faces while a skullcap measured brain activity. "When the abused children saw an angry face, their brain wave activity was dramatically stronger and longer lasting."

HALIMO—SOMALIAN REFUGEE

Our class includes a sixth-grade girl who is a refugee from Somalia. She smiles sweetly, nods, and appears to understand. She doesn't. I am told Halimo nods and appears sweetly obedient because it meant survival in the refugee camp. Halimo wants so desperately to be like the other girls, to know what the other girls know. It is difficult to understand whether her learning blocks are due to the depth of her gaps in basic developmental concepts or whether they are language blocks.

Last week I became more aware of Halimo's life story when her mother's story was printed in a women's newspaper. In 1991, when Halimo was about four years old, soldiers stormed her extended family's comfortable compound. Thirty-nine of her relatives were killed that night, including her father. Halimo, her two sisters, and infant brother escaped with their grandmother. Halimo's mother, educated in France as a nurse, was captured. During the next four years, her mother suffered unspeakable torture and abuse. When she escaped through the U.N. office, she desperately searched for information about her children and mother. Finally, her children were found in a refugee camp with their grandmother. Last spring Halimo came to the United States, along with her mother, sisters, and brother. They had to leave Grandma, who had been the children's parent

John Fauber writes in the May 12, 1999, Milwaukee Journal Sentinel about a report from the Child Emotion Research Laboratory at the University of Wisconsin-Madison that suggests that the brains of abused children are wired differently from those not abused.

"Because of their vigilance in identifying threatening cues, such children may see anger where it does not exist. And because they are preoccupied with spotting anger, they may be less able to see non-threatening expressions."

—John Fauber (1999), Milwaukee Journal Sentinel, p. 1

Studies show that every dollar spent on early childhood development programs translates into saving five dollars later in social services, mental health services, prisons, and other programs intended to deal with the aftermath of aggression and violence.
—Ronald Kotulak (1996), *Inside the Brain,* p. 44

for seven years. Halimo's mother is struggling to find a way to bring her mother to join the family.

I cannot conceive of such experiences. I cannot conceive of the terror and degradation, the inhumanity to fellow humans. The knowledge of this family's experiences enters my heart with sadness. Halimo's presence in my classroom has enriched my life and increased my commitment to make a difference in this young woman's life. Because their tragedy was so tremendous, their story has been shared by the Center for Victims of Torture. If I better understood other children's life stories, I would be better able to provide the care and insights needed to foster their growth.

I work with fraction circles to help Halimo understand how to name fractions. On this occasion, I see a glimpse of real understanding in her eyes. She glows with success, and we begin adding fractions with common denominators. I have to find Halimo more one-on-one tutoring. I teach other children in our class how to coach her with manipulatives. I find an eighth grader to tutor her on the days we have an after-school program. Halimo is hungry for a chance to succeed. I must provide the support she needs for success.

As the year continued, Halimo was able to make significant progress. She carried her Somali-English dictionary with her constantly. Math was particularly difficult because she had little background with such concepts during her years in the refugee camp. She continues to be very polite with adults. She is, however, hypervigilant to every small offense by another child. I wonder, is this a survival strategy deeply embedded within her brain chemistry?

SETH—"I'M NOT DOING NOTHING."

Seth slouches in his chair. He does as little work as possible. He is an older sixth grader who somehow, along the way, decided to play dumb. What is his story? What triggers his gaming instead of his engaging? He writes so lightly, his work is hard to read. He wastes time, his mind wandering to places unknown as he grins absently at the world. Nothing is ever his fault: "I'm not doing nothing," he responds, with paragraphs and paragraphs to explain his actions.

> *The crucial ingredient is a commitment to knowing the minds—the persons—of individual students. This means learning about each student's background, strengths, interests, preferences, anxieties, experiences, and goals, not to stereotype or to preordain but rather to ensure that educational decisions are made on the basis of an up-to-date profile of the student.*
> *—Howard Gardner (1999b),*
> *Intelligence Reframed, p. 151.*

"That's true," I respond. "I've noticed you aren't doing anything. That is the problem. It might be good to get to work. What do you think?"

I feel I have really tried to get through the demeanor, the shield he has manufactured around himself, but am making only minimal progress. What is the key? What happened? How do I unlock Seth's potential when he seems to think learning is for the teacher rather than for himself?

Today, November 10th, I had a glimmer of hope that Seth's attitude is improving. Last year, Seth began a tutoring relationship with a man in his 20s during our after-school program. That young man continued working with Seth this year. When Seth returned after tutoring today, he was smiling. I commented, "Your smile looks great, Seth. Did you accomplish a lot today?"

"Yeh," he replies. "I did."

"It looks like it feels good to accomplish a lot. Are you proud of yourself?"

He nods, flashes a big smile, and slides out the door. Inches. New self-confidence comes in inches, but I feel there is a chance for a breakthrough.

ANDY—TOO MANY CHANGES

Andy joined our classroom in the middle of last year. He was having a difficult time in his previous room. He was unfocused. He got attention as the class clown. His skills are low. He is just as likely to be making thrusting sexual maneuvers as working on a learning task.

In the beginning of this year, Andy is more settled. It feels as though he's beginning to understand that learning is for his benefit, not for me, a teacher he originally viewed as trying to make his life miserable. Slowly, ever so slowly, he shows more focus. He begins to check the record book to find out which assignments he is missing. Then he disappears. He's gone more than two weeks and we hear nothing. One bright winter morning he walks in again. Mom, he shares, decided it would be better if they lived with relatives in St. Louis, but it didn't work out, so they are back now.

In February, Andy is absent for three days, enough to give me concern. When he returns, he shares what a nice place he's living in now—Mary's Place—and gives me the phone number of his new apartment. He talks of the new kids he's met and the basketball court he plans to use. Mary's Place is a homeless shelter on the edge of downtown.

In April, Andy disappears again. This time, after a week, I get a call from the school social worker in a suburban, almost rural, district outside of Minneapolis. "Can you tell me what level of math and reading Andy is functioning at?" We chat for a while, and I find out Andy and his mom are in another shelter. His mom had a black eye when she registered Andy for school. I ask the school social worker if Andy could call me the next day and she says she will arrange it.

Andy calls. He sounds very groggy, but he's not a morning person, and it's about 8:30 a.m. We talk about his new school, a sixth- through eighth-grade school with eight periods a day. He has made one friend, a boy who happens to be in three of his classes. Everyone else is a stranger. Each class has a textbook, and he has a locker. The work is hard.

Ten days later, early on a Monday morning, I enter the building and walk into the office. There is Andy and his mom registering once again for our school. Andy is so happy to be back! He is in our classroom before the other children arrive, so I purposefully position myself to let the other children know Andy is back. Friends greet him—some with high fives, others with caution stemming from a sense of perplexity. How can Andy disappear and reappear? How is his life like mine, they wonder?

Andy has changed. He seems to be so thankful that he is back in our classroom that he is much easier to discipline. Despite missing 37 days this year, Andy finishes strong. When he stands before the class with two partners to teach the immune system, he knows his stuff. He is poised and proud. I nudge our student teacher and whisper, "If a visitor was watching Andy now, she'd never believe how much trouble he has been through!"

With the typing support of a timely parent volunteer, Andy finishes his last report. He finishes each and every assignment and is ready to fully participate in our end-of-the-year event. I ask, "Andy, what have you learned about getting your work done on time?"

He responds, "It would be a lot better if I worked every week. I know I can do it. But I have to ask questions instead of just not doing it."

This is why I teach!

Our classroom of 25 fifth and sixth graders is very diverse. The eight children I've written about represent the bright and the intellectually limited. They represent the wealthy, the middle class, and the poor. These children are typical of children in all schools. Some children move through school with ease. They tend to have appropriate personal skills. They are able to trust adults. They aren't afraid to ask questions, and they recover from mistakes. They are pliable, able to cope with the changes in our classroom. It is a joy to be with these children. But it is the other children with poor personal skills that remain in my mind. They take significantly more time and energy. And if I don't deal with their needs, their lack of skills will block the learning of the rest of the children. Our classroom is a community; each of us affects the other.

> One looks back with appreciation to brilliant teachers, but with gratitude to those who touched our human feelings. The curriculum is so much necessary raw material but warmth is the vital element for the growing plan and for the soul of the child.
> —Carl Jung in *Collected Works*, William McGuire, paragraph 249

7

Our Diversity

Respect for diversity is a "must" in a multiple-intelligence classroom. For years the concept of diversity has been dominated by issues of racial identity. Racial and cultural groups certainly have distinct issues in the United States. However, within any racial group there is extensive diversity. When I compare the wonderful personal skills of our Minneapolis School Superintendent with the abrasive personality of a Harvard-educated lawyer, I know their differences are distinctive. These two highly educated, black adults are extremely diverse! PhDs and the racial label of *black* are about all they have in common.

I have had the children from a low-income black family in my classroom—one child after the other—for six years. Their mom just successfully completed her high school equivalency exam and beams with pride. There is a gulf of difference between her life and our Superintendent of Schools. Racial diversity is one issue, an important one, but by no means the only diversity issue.

The choices teachers make about curriculum are important factors for teaching respect for diversity. I choose curriculum experience to reinforce the personal intelligences. I have state and district guidelines that define curriculum, but I also have some flexibility to decide what's best for my children. Blindly following guidelines, without reflecting on the deeper goals and needs of my particular group of children, would not be holding myself to the highest standard. My commitment is to encourage children's greatest potential. The curricular choices I make are crucial.

Each year I choose to read the picture book, *People* (Spier, 1980), to my students. The beautiful pictures and script aptly portray the diversity, the beauty, of humanity around the world. Some years I have linked this book to collecting data "about us" and have organized students into teams for surveys. This year I linked the book to issues of immigration. I asked children to identify places their ancestors lived. Students interviewed their parents about family traditions from around the world.

Children in our classroom represent every region of the world from Korea, Ireland, Poland, Denmark, Laos, Somalia, France, Peru, Chile, and more. We graphed the number of generations since our families had immigrated to the United States. Halimo, Panta, and three children adopted from other lands were our most recent immigrants.

DIVERSITY OF PERCEPTUAL STRENGTHS

Early each year, I ask students to complete a survey on their perceptual strengths—auditory, visual, kinesthetic. Knowing their strengths is important for children to gain insights on effective study strategies. A few days later, for the after-recess journal question, I ask students to reflect on study strategies: "Are you using auditory, visual, or kinesthetic strategies to learn your spelling words?" In the following meeting, we discuss their responses.

Kate shares her auditory strategy: "My mother tests me out loud. I need to hear it."

Kyle explains, "I look at the word, then I see it in my brain." He is a visual learner. Often visual spellers can picture the word and spell it frontward or backward, as Kyle can.

No one shares a kinesthetic technique, such as drawing a letter in the air with an extended arm, yet I know I have numerous children who are kinesthetic learners. I make note to work with those children, to help them use their natural style for studying spelling words.

Perceptual Modalities

Auditory: You learn easily through your ears, you remember what you hear, phonics is a good strategy for you because you are able to distinguish the differences in sounds, you probably enjoy reading aloud, and prefer to talk through a problem in order to solve it.

Visual: You learn easily through your eyes, you remember what you see, sight words are a better reading strategy for you, you can easily visualize what you read, writing lists and plans help you remember or solve problems.

Kinesthetic: You learn best by involving your whole body in an experience, you remember what you do, reading is often difficult for you because you need action rather than symbols on a page, you physically attack a problem rather than talk about it.

I continue, "Should all of you use the same method of studying?"

A resounding, "NO."

"Why?"

They know very well, but I want to emphasize that we are all different and we are all just fine. I am modeling respect for their diversity of perceptual styles.

EXTRAVERSION AND INTROVERSION

A few days later, with a show of hands, I use the *Psychology for Kids* (Kincher, 1990) inventory, which identifies preferences for Extraversion or Introversion. Students make two columns and simply tally their preferences. We discuss background information on their Extravert/Introvert preferences. I use this opportunity to teach a double-sided bar graph on the chalkboard. The instrument has 15 questions. Thus, I start a number line at 15 in descending order to 9, an even score. On the top of the line, I record Introverted preferences, below, the Extraverted. It doesn't surprise me that 12 of our students claim preference to be high Extraverts and only 5 claim high Introversion.

Introvert/Extravert Preferences

15	14	13	12	11	10	9	8	
				X				
			X	X	X	X		Introvert
		X		X	X	X	X	Extravert
		X		X	X		X	
	X		X					
			X					

Seven children have scores that are about even, with both scores under nine points. I probe, "What kind of person is the 'right' kind of person?" I continue to model. There is no right and wrong. There are preferences, but preferences are not an excuse to be rude or disrespectful to others. Once again, I point out our diversity and reinforce respect for each of us.

GRAPHING DIVERSITY

The following week, when I teach a math lesson on changing fractions to decimals to percentages, I choose to use my students' diversity as the data. Students' brains are naturally engaged when I focus on their lives. I ask the children to draw a circle in their math journals as I draw on the chalkboard. "This circle represents all of us," I explain. "It's 100%. If I divide you into two groups, it's half of you." I divide the circle and write "1/2." "A dollar has 100 cents; how much is half a dollar?" I am linking to their prior knowledge at a level all listeners can participate. "Right. Fifty cents is the same as 50%. What if I divided you into four groups? If you divide a dollar into four groups, how much is in a group?" I ask them to draw a circle into fourths and write the fraction, the decimal, and the percent.

Extraverts, with their need for sociability, appear to be energized, or "tuned up," by people. Talking to people, playing with people, and working with people is what charges their batteries.

Introverts need to find quiet places and solitary activities to recharge, while these activities exhaust the extravert.

—David Keirsey and Marilyn Bates (1978), Please Understand Me, pp. 14, 15

One of the most important concepts for a 5-year-old to know is that he or she can teach because you have to understand something to teach it.
—Marian Diamond, "The Brains Behind the Brain," *Educational Leadership,* p. 21

We are ready to use real data. I know for some of my children this lesson will be a review, and for others it is a totally new concept, so I pair students, new with experienced as teacher helpers. I expect children to teach each other; it reinforces their own thoughts.

Math journals are out, pairs are settled in, and calculators are distributed. I ask, "How many students are in the room right now? 24. And how many of you are boys? Girls? The total number is the down number, the denominator. The number of boys is the numerator, it goes on top. Write the two fractions, for boys and girls, in your journal. Add the top numbers. What do you get?" I continue by demonstrating on the chalkboard how to divide the fraction to get a decimal, then how to do it on the calculator. The children decide to use their calculators to divide (a reasonable decision on their part). Finally we change the form to percent and I demonstrate how to use the circle graph template to create a 100% circle with two parts, the boys and the girls.

Numerous parents of adopted children requested that their children be in a class with other adopted children. Thus, our classroom has seven adopted children. We are fortunate to be able to talk openly about what makes a family, so I continue the math lesson by asking the adopted children to raise their hands. We go through the process of writing out the two fractions, decimals, percent, and a circle graph. I ask who lives with one parent and who with two parents, and repeat the process. I continue with more data questions such as, "Who has a pet?"

The children are doing this level easily now so I add another layer of complexity by graphing three fractions. "Remember when we did the Extravert/Introvert survey? Some of you were clearly one or the other, some of you were in the middle. Raise your hand if you were in the middle. That's seven of you. Write the fraction, 7/24. How many of you were Introverts? Extraverts? Make the circle graph using all three fractions." Our next circle graph is on auditory, visual, and kinesthetic preferences. I continue on, using data on who likes pizza, tacos, or hamburgers the best, and the students make another graph. Our final graph is who likes gym, music, or art the best.

In this math lesson I developed intrapersonal and interpersonal skills by using helping partners. I taught fraction-decimal-percent concepts. Children developed calculator skills and used the circle graph template. I made our diversity center stage, affirming the children's lives. The experience took about 45 minutes. My curriculum choices make a difference in children's lives.

SELF-MANAGEMENT/IMPULSE CONTROL

One area of significant diversity is self-management. Emotional self-management first requires being aware of one's emotions. Emotional self-management is needed for delayed gratification. Self-management is the opposite of impulsivity. Impulse control is particularly important because emotions create the impulse to act. The word *emotion* comes from the Latin root *to move*. Emotional self-management is necessary to move to more complex tasks. Impulse control is a major issue for many children who are struggling with academic learning.

The "Marshmallow Test" is the classic study of impulse control. This study began in the 1960s. It evaluated four-year-olds' ability to resist eating a marshmallow when the researcher was out of the room. On the videotape we see some children covered their eyes so they wouldn't have to look at the temptation. Other children talked to themselves, sang, or played with the marshmallow. Some children immediately grabbed the marshmallow as soon as the adult left the room.

Twelve to 14 years later, these children's lives were evaluated. Goleman (1998) writes,

> The emotional and social difference between the grab-the-marshmallow preschoolers and their gratification-delaying peers was dramatic. Those who had resisted temptation at four were now, as adolescents, more socially competent: personally effective, self-assertive, and better able to cope with the frustrations of life. They were less likely to go to pieces, freeze, or regress under stress, or become rattled and disorganized when pressured; they embraced challenges and pursued them instead of giving up even in the face of difficulties; they were self-reliant and confident, trustworthy and dependable; and they took initiative and plunged into projects.

The third or so who grabbed for the marshmallow, however, tended to have fewer of these qualities, and shared instead a relatively more troubled psychological portrait. In adolescence they were more likely to be seen as shying away from social contacts; to be stubborn and indecisive; to be easily upset by frustrations; to think of themselves as "bad" or unworthy; to regress or become immobilized by stress; to be mistrustful and resentful about not "getting enough"; to be prone to jealously and envy; to overreact to irritations with a sharp temper, so provoking arguments and fights. And, after all those years, they still were unable to put off gratification. (pp. 81, 82)

It turned out that how children did on this delayed-gratification test was a powerful predictor of their SAT scores. The children who had waited were better students. They scored higher on both the verbal and math SAT tests than the marshmallow-grabbing children. Poor impulse control was a predictor of problem behaviors.

To ensure children's success I must help children learn to deal with impulsivity and develop the ability to delay gratification. Most impulsive children aren't aware of what they are doing. They don't seem to reflect on how they are feeling. I ask my students, "How do you feel today? What does your body feel like when you're happy? When you're stressed?" Too often children don't register what they are feeling until they are overwhelmed and act impulsively.

I want children to be aware of the messages of their emotions. I want children to link words to their body states. "My stomach is tight. My shoulders are tense. Why am I uncomfortable? Is someone threatening me, treating me badly, or attacking me with criticism?" Learning to be self-aware is a complex process, yet without self-awareness you can't deal with impulsiveness. The child must sense her body's messages, label the sense with words, and then determine the meaning of the message, before action.

MINDFULNESS

Becoming "mindful" is an important aspect of self-awareness. Mindfulness brings an awareness of our attention and intention. Joseph slouches in his seat; he is physically in the room but he is not really here. He isn't aware that he isn't attending. He doesn't know he isn't tuned in. Because he doesn't know, he feels unjustly picked on when I try to refocus his attention. "I'm listening," he claims. Unfortunately, there is a big difference between hearing and listening.

> *Our frontal lobes play an especially important role in that they control, fixate, and shift our conscious attention—thus determining what's foreground and background, and how the current situation relates to our previous experience.*
> *—Robert Sylwester (1997a), A Celebration of Neurons, p. 79*

Tuning in mindfully is a conscious process. Many teachers feel children are more tuned out than ever before. In the mid-1960s, when I began teaching, most children stayed tuned in—even though I was an unskilled teacher. Within the last 8 years, more and more children are having difficulty tuning in mindfully. Is the tuned-out-ness caused by increased viewing of TV, video, and computer games? I wonder. It is clear to me that schoolchildren's natural focusing has decreased.

To focus attention, we must be able to distinguish between important and irrelevant stimuli, then ignore the irrelevant. At the same time, our minds must tap into relevant memories and connect to previous experiences and understandings. To do this, our frontal lobes must shift rapidly—linking and attending—to maintain focus.

Ellen Langer has written extensively on mindfulness. In *The Power of Mindful Learning,* she cites extensive evidence that mindfulness can be learned. Once mindfulness is learned it facilitates all other learning. The process of learning how to focus is clearly part of intrapersonal management.

We know the mind is always scanning for changes. When something new happens, the brain naturally takes notice. Langer (1997) explains,

> *Since many children with attention problems in other settings can remain glued to a screen for extended time periods, their computer use requires special care, and some researchers are already pursuing this challenge. I expect computers will eventually lay new routes to good habits. Above all, we want our young people to be in charge of their own mental habits, not so mentally scattered that they are at the mercy of each passing impulse or sensation.*
> *—Jane Healy (1998), Failure to Connect, p. 184*

The most effective way to increase our ability to pay attention is to look for the novelty within the stimulus situation, whether it is a story, a map, or a painting. This is the most useful lesson to teach our children, because it enables them to be relatively independent of other people and of their physical environment. If novelty (and interest) is in the mind of other people and of their physical environment. If novelty (and interest) is in the mind of the attender, it doesn't matter that a teacher presents the same old things or tells us to sit still and concentrate in a fixed manner. (p. 43)

Usually, by age seven children have developed selective attention. The period between ages seven and nine is particularly important in developing mindful attention. The child needs to learn to focus attention, reflect on actions, and make judgments to form an organized plan. Joseph hasn't made it through this brain development stage. As a sixth grader he often isn't aware of where his mind is. When I ask what his plan is, that is, what are his reflections that will create his action, his typical response is, "I donno." Is he just trying to be a wise-off? I don't think so. How do I cope with him? Somehow, I have to encourage his internal attention and therefore, in the midst of many other things, I try to check in with him. "What are you thinking about, Joseph?" "What is the next thing you are going to do?"

> There are two levels of emotions, conscious and unconscious. The moment of an emotion coming into awareness means it's registering as such in the frontal cortex.
> —Daniel Goleman (1998), *Emotional Intelligence*, p. 55

I know enough about stages of brain development to understand some of the processes of children learning to focus their attention, but my remedial strategies are like fledglings.

Attention Deficit Hyperactivity Disorder—ADHD

Impulsiveness has become a national issue linked to the million kids diagnosed as having attention deficit hyperactivity disorder (ADHD). In my class of fifth and sixth graders, four very bright boys are ADHD. Boys are significantly more likely to be identified as ADHD. They attend to the smallest changes around them, and the changes distract them. They seem unable to sort out relevant and irrelevant stimuli to stay focused. Their attention switches to irrelevant stimuli, and they lose track of what they are supposed to be accomplishing. ADHD, or ADD, isn't an attention deficit. It is the opposite. Children with ADD attend to everything rather than maintaining a selected focus.

The prefrontal cortex is involved in the reflective process-ing of emotions. It is the "executive brain" because of its role in decision making. This area continues to mature through young adulthood, maybe into our 40s. It monitors internal speech, which provides direction toward goals: "What do I need to do now? Should I do this next?" The executive functions of the prefrontal cortex deal with organizing thoughts, deciding pri-orities, and choosing strategies. The prefrontal cortex provides guidance through self-monitoring and sorts relevant/irrele-vant stimulus. Without self-monitoring, achieving goals is quite difficult. In children with ADD and ADHD, the mecha-nism for staying focused, the work of dopamine in the prefrontal cortex, doesn't seem to function within a "normal" range.

ADHD has a developmental component, which researchers label "neurodevelopmental lag." This lag is reflected in the social-emotional skills of children with ADD, behaving two to three years younger than their age. They often overreact in emo-tional situations. They speed up when stressed rather than us-ing reflective, evaluative thought processes.

Neurological assessments provide insights on the differ-ences in ADD and "normal" brains. At the National Institute of Mental Health, researchers found high levels of dopamine in the cerebrospinal fluid of hyperactive boys. In another study, PET scans on adults with ADHD showed decreased frontal lobe metabolism. MRI studies have documented ADHD males with both a decreased blood flow in the right caudate of their basil ganglia and a right caudate that was 3% smaller than males without ADHD.

Clearly, there is diversity in my children's brains. Some fo-cus their attention easily; others do not. Some use reflective, evaluative thinking; others do not. Some children take in infor-mation easily in more than one perceptual modality. The diver-sity of my students' brains may be greater than we've ever imag-ined and, through research, we are learning more each day.

LEARNING WHO WE ARE—MBTI

Awareness of our diversity—awareness of ourselves and oth-ers—is an important factor of personal intelligence. When I gained awareness that I am a visual learner, I understood why I had trouble learning in lectures. Because I understand my body rhythm, it was clear that to write this book, I would need to get up early in the morning when my thoughts are the sharpest. The first time I took the Myers-Briggs Type Indicator (MBTI), I gasped with surprise, "How do they know that about me?"

When information about learning styles began to enter our conversations about education, it was an issue for the teacher. The teacher needed to have learning-style insights to differentiate instructional strategies. I suggest that it is crucial for each learner to understand his or her style. It is the learner who must "know oneself" to be an advocate for herself. A visual learner, like myself, needs to know coping skills for lectures and use mind mapping to be able to "see" the information. An Extravert, like my daughter, needs to find study partners to discuss ideas. It is very important for students, and also for teachers, to understand their learning styles. Understanding and respecting our differences is a critical part of personal intelligence.

The student version of the MBTI is the Murphy-Meisgeiger Type Indicator for Children (MMTIC). This instrument is a powerful tool for self-understanding. It gives my fifth and sixth graders the language to identify differences and value our individual uniqueness. Over the years, I've found that parents are eager to understand their child's preferences.

Extraversion and Introversion

The MBTI and MMTIC use letter codes to represent preferences in four dichotomies. The first preference determined by the MBTI and MMTIC is the quality that refers to our basic attitude toward life—Extraversion and Introversion (the "E" and "I"). Extraverts focus energy on their external world; Introverts on their internal world. I am a strong Introvert. My idea of a good day is to have quiet time to reflect on how I feel and what I believe. Near my computer, I have posted a quote by David Hare: "The act of writing is the act of discovering what you believe." Writing is one way I reflect on my thoughts. In contrast, my 22-year-old daughter is a raving Extravert. Her idea of a good day is to have a continuous flow of action and interactions, people and the phone, but not quiet time. Quiet time is deadly.

About 65% of Americans are Extraverts. They think out loud by talking about their ideas. In classrooms, Extraverts may answer before their hands go up. Learning alone is difficult for Extraverts because talking helps them think, just as writing helps me think.

Sensing and Intuition

The second pair of MBTI preferences refers to functions. "S" represents the sensing function, and "N" represents the intuition function (because "I" already represents "Introvert"). Sensors (people who prefer sensing) make up about 70% of our population. The younger the child, the greater the likelihood he is a sensor. Developmentally, the child is storing sensory memories to build an understanding of his physical world. These children notice the sensory details and like specific directions.

In a study of 500 people who dropped out of school in the eighth grade, 99% were sensors. Because sensors rely on learning from their senses, it is crucial that they are provided with stimulation in their strongest sensory modality. The dominant senses for education are auditory, visual, and kinesthetic. If a student is a strong kinesthetic sensor and the teacher is lecturing, the student will have a very difficult time learning. The student must have sensory input in the way that she is best able to process it. It is my responsibility to help sensor students understand which strategies work best for them.

For the last five years, I have had the opportunity of working with master's candidates from the University of Minnesota, College of Education. I give them a self-report perceptual modality inventory. Most of these college students turn out to be auditory learners. They have been successful in lecture classes. They also tend to think that others learn by hearing. Most young children, however, are kinesthetic learners. They must do to learn. Developmentally, young children are first kinesthetic learners. As their visual cortex develops, some children may become visual learners and some may become

come auditory learners and others visual. Auditory is the last to mature, but that does not mean kinesthetic or visual learners are somehow less intelligent.

I am a visual learner. I can write a grocery list, forget it at home, and still remember almost everything I need to buy. Secondly, I am a kinesthetic learner. I need to experience to learn. Auditory is my least effective sense. I hear just fine, but I don't discriminate or remember using my auditory sense. I am a perfectly smart person, but I still do not learn using phonics—phonics is an auditory sequential process.

People with a preference for intuition represent about 30% of the population. It is rare to find a very young child who is truly intuitive because we must have sensory experiences to make the connection—the hunches—typical of an intuition.

A few years ago, I had the opportunity to experience a summer internship processing brain PET (positron emission tomography) scans. One morning when I arrived at the site, in the basement of a large medical complex, the usually jovial top researcher, Dr. Jose Pardo, was pacing and storming. "What's going on?" I asked a co-worker. This procedure, he explained, was to pinpoint brain areas for different auditory tones, but the subject was not showing auditory discrimination. Her visual cortex was being activated! I thought of children I taught and asked, rather quietly, "Do you know if she is a visual learner?"

Later, when debriefing, I again mentioned that I have visual learners, auditory learners, kinesthetic learners, and all of the resulting combinations. I explained how I use a simple hands-on activity to determine which perceptual modality is the child's strongest. The reaction was essentially, Yah, sure. These folks were researching with a multimillion-dollar machine and I had a hands-on kit to determine perceptual modality.

Well, I went to school and got our modality kit. I called the woman to come back and take the modality evaluation and, sure enough, she was a strong visual learner. "I can't remember anything by just hearing it," she said, "so I automatically make pictures so I can see it." She was efficiently taking auditory stimuli and creating visuals that increased her memories.

The modality kit is handled by Zaner-Bloser Company.

make the connection—the hunches—typical of an intuition. Intuitive people tend to invent, to focus on the possibilities, to initiate and promote. They tend to skip over directions, focusing on the main idea but forgetting the details. They "read between the lines," seeing the big picture. They are drawn toward the future. A study of National Merit Finalists found 83% of the students were intuitive. Intuitives have an easier time in our schools.

Thinking and Feeling

The next pair of MBTI preferences refer to how we make decisions—the Thinking and Feeling ("T" and "F") functions. Again, there is no right or wrong, neither is better. Half of us are Thinkers, making decisions based on cause and effect, standards, analysis, and principles that seem to be objective. The Thinker is often good at evaluating and criticizing, sometimes alienating others.

Half of us are Feelers, preferring to make our decisions based on emotional content. "If I do this, she will probably get angry." I purposefully remember to greet my Feelers each morning, or they will decide I'm angry at them. Because my Feelers are tuned to emotions, I must be sure they are calm so they can learn.

Judging and Perceiving

The last group of the MBTI preferences indicates how we prefer to interact with our outer world. Judging and Perceiving ("J" and "P") are also 50-50%. Judgers have an easy time meeting deadlines and accommodating schedules. These are the students who turn assignments in on time. They like to finish one project at a time, then set a new goal. They seem organized and prepared. They like to make decisions and run things.

Perceivers live in the present. Their strengths are being fully in the moment, not planning ahead. They are flexible and spontaneous and they handle changes well. They prefer schoolwork that is game-like and playful. Most younger students are perceivers. Teachers need to coach perceivers by helping them "plan backwards." "Julie, your assignment is due on Thursday. What are you doing Wednesday evening? Oh, you're playing soccer. What are you doing Tuesday? Can you finish the work on Tuesday?"

The Dunn and Dunn Research

All types are created equal. By this we mean that no type is better or worse than any other type. However, all types have unique strengths and possible weaknesses. And typically, the greatest strength of one type is very often the biggest blind spot of the opposite type.
—Paul Tieger and Barbara Barron-Tieger (1997), Nurture by Nature, p. 39

Another factor of knowing oneself is knowing your environmental, emotional, sociological, and physiological preferences. Our diversity in these areas was first researched by Rita and Ken Dunn in the 1970s.

Environment factors include your preference to work in silence or with background music, in bright light or dim light, your preference for having a room warm or cool, and whether you prefer to work at a desk (table) or more informally sitting in a big chair or sofa. I ask teachers, "Where do you feel best when working? Where are you the most productive?" Where you work is not right or wrong; it is a preference.

The Dunns' extensive research predicts that if you are in the conditions you prefer, you do better. If you prefer to have background music, you accomplish more with background music. Likewise, our students have environmental preferences. Some students wear T-shirts throughout our Minnesota winters; others bundle up in many layers. Some students always head for the couch in my classroom meeting area; others always choose a table. When students have the environment that makes them feel comfortable, they learn more effectively.

The Dunns also looked at sociological preferences. They found some learners prefer to have adults close by, others do not. Some students prefer to work alone (probably the Introverts), whereas others prefer to have a partner or work with a small group (probably the Extraverts). Regardless, students who studied with their preference—alone or with others—learned more efficiently.

In addition, the Dunns' research identified four physical aspects of learning styles: modality (auditory, visual, kinesthetic), intake (the preference to snack or have three meals), time of day (morning peak time, evening peak time), and mobility (the need to move around while learning or the desire to sit still).

It is important to recognize and respect these elements of preferred style. As I began writing this book, I realized how little I was able to accomplish in the evenings; my mind was clogged from the day's activities. However, I am naturally alert as soon as I wake. Thus, I set my alarm for 5:00 a.m. and wrote for an hour and a half before I dressed for school. When my thoughts got blocked and I didn't know what to write next, I would get up and do something around the house—put the laundry in the washer or scrape the dishes, for example. I would sit back down at the computer and, magically, I would understand what to do next. For me, a bit of movement clears my head and rejuvenates my focus. Organizing my work with respect for my style increases my efficiency and productivity.

Eight Multiple Intelligences

Obviously, our diversity is shown in our aptitude for the eight multiple intelligences. (Because this book focuses on Gardner's concept of multiple intelligence, I deal with it only briefly in this section.) Niko excels in math. Steffi writes beautiful poetry. Maggie plays the violin in the city-side youth orchestra. Kyle's sketches are outstanding. Sydney plays a tough

The Eight Intelligences: Verbal linguistic, Logical mathematical, Bodily kinesthetic, Visual spatial, Musical rhythmic, Naturalist, Intrapersonal, and Interpersonal. The criteria for defining intelligence:

1. The potential of isolation by brain damage.

2. An evolutionary history and evolutionary plausibility.

3. An identifiable core operation or set of operations.

4. Susceptibility to encoding in a symbol system.

5. A distinct developmental history, along with a definable set of expert "end-state" performances.

6. The existence of idiot savants, prodigies, and other exceptional people.

7. Support from experimental psychological tasks.

8. Support from psychometric findings.

—Howard Gardner (1999b), *Intelligence Reframed,* pp. 36-40

game of soccer. The diversity of our intelligences is easy to identify and is important. We need all of our intelligences for the richness of this world. We need the Maya Angelous. We need the Einstiens. We need Jacque Coustous. We need Babe Ruths. We need Leonardo da Vinci, Bach, Mother Teresa, and Helen Keller. Our world needs all of the eight intelligences in the orchestra of life.

8

Nurturing Independence

I teach reading. I teach math. But I don't think of myself as a reading/math teacher. I like the title "specialist in developing children." I help brains grow. I nurture new dendrite connections in all children.

Two of my fifth graders, Niko and Kyndra, are strong introverts. That's about the only thing they have in common. Their brains are extremely different. Purposefully, there is no TV in Niko's home. His mother is an artist. His father teaches physics at the university. Niko reads at an adult level and plays the guitar. He scored in the 99th percentile on national tests. The world makes sense to him. He functions well.

In Kyndra's home the TV is a constant. Mom's life seems to be experienced via stories on the TV. The TV seems to be doing the thinking. Kyndra is a beginning reader. Often she misses the meaning of words because she has such limited experience that it is difficult to connect to her prior knowledge. National tests place Kyndra in the 9th percentile. How differently these two children approach life!

It is important that I support Niko's achievement by providing him with a safe and stimulating environment. He

For children from less verbal environments, including middle- and upper-income homes where screen time substitutes for family conversations, this (inner voice) development may be delayed. Inner speech is important to academic as well as personal development. From ages six to nine, gains in math achievement as well as in other subjects are related to the use of self-talk ("How should I do this problem—oh, I think I'll try . . .").
—Jane Healy (1998), *Failure to Connect*, p. 233

has so many things going for him. On Mondays, I often observe Niko in front of the assignment board making notes in his datebook, planning his week so he can finish everything in a timely fashion. Niko is able to cooperate interpersonally as needed. His solid intrapersonal self-management and emotional stability is obvious. He is already an independent learner.

It took me quite a while to begin to unlock Kyndra's potential. She was used to going through the motions of learning, without learning. Subtraction was difficult for her. We worked, repeatedly, with the ones-tens-hundreds blocks until she internalized trading and regrouping. Kyndra had approached math as a rote activity rather than understanding what she was doing. (Our math computational program is differentiated. Niko has completed all topics in pre-algebra.) Once Kyndra learned subtraction, she did the same pages over and over. "Kyndra, you can't get credit for the same page over and over. You need to move on to something a bit harder." We have a class saying—you have to work "hard enough but not too hard." This is our interpretation of L. S. Vygotsky's concept of the "zone of proximal development." What is hard enough for Kyndra is certainly too easy for Niko. What was hard enough for Kyndra last week should be too easy this week. However, Kyndra stayed stuck. She knew how to do subtraction, so that's what she did.

For me, there is simply no choice. I have to juggle the pre-algebra assignments for Niko and the hands-on subtraction for Kyndra. Both need to think about what they are doing; both need to reflect on what they are learning. Each needs to feel emotionally satisfied with working hard. Niko knows when he's stretched his dendrites and learned a new idea. He has internal talk to congratulate himself. Kyndra needed to learn how to give herself positive internal messages and notice successes.

Slowly, we made progress. Kyndra started talking with me about her life. She started sharing, just a bit at a time. Talking with Kyndra gave me a chance to link her thinking to new ideas. Kyndra had a history of missing many days of school. By midyear, she learned to take public transportation and came to school even when she missed the school bus. This was an important step. She was beginning to feel responsible for her own life. Even if she came an hour late, I warmly welcomed her. "Good to have you here, Kyndra!" Small steps. Important steps.

Ruby Payne makes the distinction between generational poverty and situational poverty. "Situational poverty is defined as a lack of resources attributable to a particular event, i.e., a death, chronic illness, divorce, etc. Generational poverty has its own culture, hidden rules, and belief systems. . . . In generational poverty, issues of language, emotional responses, role models, and knowledge of tacit social rules are often significant blocks to success in school."
—*Ruby Payne (1995), A Framework for Understanding and Working with Students and Adults from Poverty, pp. 102, 16*

The words I use, when talking with children, are very important. I wanted to expand Kyndra's thought patterns. "I notice you're doing your subtraction faster now,"I tell Kyndra. I use the word "notice" because I want her to start noticing what she is doing. I sit with her as she begins to write a story. "Have you noticed in storybooks that they indent paragraphs? Look," I demonstrate with a book, "each time there's a change there is an indent—a dent in at the beginning of the line. Let's look at your writing and you tell me when there is a change." I mark some of her paragraphs as a model and she returns to her writing. Our talk was gentle. It was relevant—she had just started writing her story. And, it was personal. Kyndra has been a passive, low-achieving student for many years. I want her to believe that I will help her, and she can learn.

Slowly, I teach Kyndra to use more thoughtful strategies of intrapersonal self-management. By the end of the year, Kyndra has become more self-directed. She is completing her homework. She is asking for help more often when she is stuck. She worked diligently sewing an emotion felt doll, much like Powerfull. Her end-of-the-year portfolio project was outstanding. I had given Kyndra a lot of attention and she had achieved significantly. In fact, at her year-end special education conference, her scores indicated she was overachieving, compared to her previous work.

Examples of Self-Instructions Students Can Learn to Use

Defining the Problem (sizing up the nature and demands of the task):
- What is it I have to do here?
- Let me see if I understand what I have to do.
- What is the problem?
- What is my goal or the way I want it to be?

Accessing and Summarizing Relevant Information:
- Have I seen a problem like this in the past?
- What do I already know about this?
- How is this like what I've done before?
- What additional information do I need?

Focusing Attention and Planning:
- I have to . . . (pay attention, concentrate, think of different ways to solve this problem).
- First, I need to make a plan.
- My first step is . . ., then I will . . .

Self-Monitoring (evaluating performance, catching and correcting errors):
- Am I following my plan? Am I ready to take the next step?
- Have I used all my story parts?
- Can I think of more details?
- I need to go slowly and take my time.
- Is this making sense?
- How am I doing? Do I need to do anything differently?

Using Coping Self-Statements (handling difficulties and figures and the accompanying reactions):
- Oops! I missed one. That's okay, I can . . . (redo it, ask for help, etc.).
- So I made an error—that's okay. I can learn from my mistake.
- I can do this if I try.
- I'm not going to get mad. Mad makes me do bad.

Self-Reinforcing (including self-attribution statements):
- How did I do? Not bad! I used my strategy to . . .
- Although I didn't get it all done, I tried hard. This was challenging.
- I am getting better at this.
- Wait until I show this to . . . (read this to . . ., etc.).
- I am proud of what I accomplished so far.

SOURCE: Adapted from *Nurturing Independent Learners*, Meichhenbaum, D. & Biemiller, A. (1998). Used with permission from Brookline Books, Cambridge, MA.

Rubric for Written Reports

Report Name: _____ Created by: _____
Evaluator's Name: _____ Date: _____ Total Points: _____

Points	5	4	3	2	1	0
Cover	Has title, author, color, relevent picture, is neat, is interesting		Missing something, or is messy		Has only title and author	Missing
Table of Contents	Correct pages, uses . . . to numbers, uses capital letters on first word, spelling is correct		Some mistakes in numbers, page setup, punctuation, or spelling		Is sloppy or misnumbered	Missing
Introduction	Page is clearly titled, on a separate page, tells what you will write about in correct order, is interesting		Has first sentence correct and mentions topics in the right order but is boring		Is too short and does not mention topics in the right order	Missing
Topic Sentences	Tells what each topic is; each is on a new page; sentences are interesting		Topic sentences are all about the same, uninteresting		Topic sentences are short with some mistakes	Missing
Spelling and Punctuation	No mistakes		Less than 10 errors in the report		Has 10-20 errors	Over 20 errors
Quality	Topic is rich with interesting descriptions in student's own words, flows easily from idea to idea		Information is good but does not flow well, sometimes sounds like it is copied from books		Information does not cover important areas of the topic	
Illustrations	5 or more relevent graphics integrated neatly, with source notes		Has less than 5 pictures, they do not have relevance, missing source notes		Few pictures which aren't neat or noted	Missing
Conclusion	What you have learned is clearly expressed		Sentences have little meaning			Missing
Bibliography	3 or more sources, alphabetized and in correct format: Last name, first. *Title*. City, State: Publisher, Date.		Less than 3 sources, problems with correct format for bibliography			Missing

Will Kyndra ever catch up on a par with Niko? No, but her potential has increased. She's thinking about herself now rather than simply going through the motions. Self-regulating learners make plans, they watch their progress, ask for help when appropriate, and relate new learning to what they already know. This takes active inner speech. I look forward to working with both Niko and Kyndra next year—Niko, a self-assured high-achieving sixth grader with great foundations in the personal intelligences, and Kyndra, as I watch her make significant strides toward increased self-management.

RUBRICS

Rubrics can be very helpful in nurturing children's independence. Each year, students in my room do three complex research reports using note cards and topic sentences. Our rubric makes the factors of a good report perfectly clear. When students have rubrics to guide their performance, they can self-evaluate. Students aren't being measured on some mysterious magical system known only to the teacher. They know the criteria for excellence. The rubric becomes the planning guide, and students check that they have all of the components. When a child has missed a component and turned in the report, I simply conference with him and ask if he'd like the report back to complete it. Usually, children are willing. They have an internal desire to be "winners."

CONTENT, COLLABORATION, AND CHOICE

The three Cs identified by Alfie Kohn (1993) in *Punished by Rewards*—content, collaboration, and choice—resonate with the development of personal intelligences, as do issues of intrinsic motivation. Extrinsic motivation means the child is doing a task for a reward. The children I teach will work hard to finish assignments to be qualified to go to the school's roller skating event, yet I use such extrinsic rewards just three times a year. Intrinsic motivation, working for one's own satisfaction, is better aligned with the intrapersonal growth I want children to experience.

I am responsible for the same content as other fifth/sixth-grade teachers in my district. Yet, because of my understanding of the personal intelligences, my focus is quite different. Choice is a big factor in how the content is taught in my classroom. Spelling illustrates the relationship of content and choice. I organize the children into cooperative group three-somes. The children create their own spelling lists—words

"In Japanese elementary schools, the three R's are underlined by the three C's: connection, character, and content. . . . Japanese elementary teachers tell us their first job is to help children develop a strong, positive emotional connection to school." Developing character includes "reflecting on one's life," "having the courage to do what one believes is right," "trusting others," "being considerate and kind," "having a heart that is moved by things beautiful and noble," "actively participate in the groups in one's daily life . . . cooperating and taking initiative to be responsible." Content, the third C, is limited. They believe "less is more." The Japanese eighth grade science textbooks cover eight topics, compared to more than 65 in American textbooks. (Lewis & Tsucida, 1998, pp. 32-24)

Seven Central Qualities of Japanese Education for Young Children

1. Focus on the Whole Child

2. Emphasis on Prosocial Values

3. Building a Supportive Community in the Classroom

4. Methods of Discipline That Promote a Personal Commitment to Values

5. Children's Thinking, Problem Solving, and Discussion Help Drive Classroom Life

6. "Wet" Learning: A "wet" approach is personal, emotional, and interpersonally complex compared to a "dry" approach, which is rational, logical, and unemotional.

7. Reflection (*Hansei*): "Children reflected, in their small groups, on whether they had worked well. Children reflected individually on their personal goals for self-improvement." (Lewis, 1995, pp. 203-207)

they didn't know when writing, words we're using in class (for example, ocean words), or other interesting words from a dictionary. Children who have "learned helplessness" have difficulty even creating a list. For other children, it is an opportunity to investigate new vocabulary. On Monday, children turn in their lists and I check for accuracy. On Wednesday, in round-robin fashion, the threesomes give each other a practice test, and on Friday, they take the final test. This system allows each child to work at a content level that is "hard enough but not too hard." Children who find spelling difficult are not shut out by this process—the content is manageable. Children who find spelling easy are challenged by further developing their vocabulary. The spelling groups change five or six times during the year, thus facilitating cooperation/collaboration between many different children in our class.

Content choice and collaboration are possible with any large topic. When we studied the human body, different groups of children taught the whole class about a particular system. The digestive-system group decided to mix crackers and milk in a baggie to illustrate what happens in our stomachs, and they also measured the hall to illustrate the length of our intestines (21 feet). Another group created a system of red dye in tubes and used a hand pump to illustrate the rhythm of our circulatory system. When the groups taught, we all learned. Children experienced many levels of interpersonal decision making. For those children with good intrapersonal skills, this collaboration is usually great fun. For children without well-developed self-management, collaboration is difficult.

Learned helplessness is a sense that "nothing I do matters; it won't change what happens to me." Children who have learned helplessness feel a lack of control over the circumstances in their lives. They are hesitant to make choices because they are convinced it won't matter anyway. "I'll still be dumb." "They still won't like me." From their point of view, it's not about the amount of their effort to improve, it's just the way life is. Understandably this emotional state changes the chemistry of their bodies, just as depression changes the body's chemistry.

Similarly, a period in history can be separated with different cooperative groups researching different topics. This year we needed to study the period of the U.S. western expansion. Groups uncovered (rather than covered) a depth of information on the trails that brought people west, the difference in landforms along the trails, the jobs of cowboys, the gold rush, the lives of Native Americans, and more. Content is focused, but varied. Children have choices related to how they find information and how they present what they have learned. In the process, they are collaborating with others.

> The brain is innately social and collaborative. Although the processing takes place in our students' individual brains, their learning is enhanced when the environment provides them with the opportunity to discuss their thinking out loud, to bounce their ideas off their peers, and to produce collaborative work.
> —Pat Wolfe and Ron Brandt (1998), "What Do We Know From Brain Research?" in *Educational Leadership*, p. 11

Do I have to teach children how to collaborate? Yes, I do a lot of coaching. Collaboration is a critical tool for students, and you learn by doing. Children get stubborn with their own ideas. They don't listen to each other. They expect another child to have the same skills as they do and become frustrated if the other child is not doing "his share." But these problems arise with adults also. It takes practice to become skilled at working in collaboration, and the only way to practice is to practice.

I am not in the business of "controlling" children, although I still need to set limits. I provide experiences for children to learn. Learning how to treat someone else is often harder than learning how to spell. In the process of learning collaboration, students have the opportunity to learn more about empathy.

EMPATHY

Respect for our diversity and empathy are linked. The word *empathy* is from the Greek *empatheia,* meaning "feeling into."

Empathy is a highly complex, emotional skill that begins in infancy. Infants, even before they realize they exist apart from other people, are affected by another child's tears in "sympathetic distress."

When an infant experiences a sense of connection and care with a parent, "attunement" develops. The mother makes eye

The truth is that if we want children to take responsibility for their own behavior, we must first give them responsibility, and plenty of it. The way a child learns how to make decisions is by making decisions, not by following directions.
—Alfie Kohn (1993), *Punished by Rewards*, p. 249

contact; the baby coos in response. The baby's emotional needs are met. Unfortunately, when a mother is depressed or unable to pick up nonverbal messages, the three-month-old child will mirror the mother's moods. Babies of depressed moms are sadder and show less interest in their world.

True empathy—the ability to feel concern for a person based on how you would feel in his circumstances—requires advanced levels of emotional development. A child must accurately read another's emotion and connect it to his or her own previous experiences. Understanding another's experience is even more complex across cultures, requiring understanding cultural differences and values.

How does this process of developing empathy play out in my classroom? An initial step in connecting emotions and ideas is teaching emotional vocabulary. A child can't connect ideas and emotions without the vocabulary. There must be a context for his thinking. We need to provide daily opportunities to discuss feelings.

The morning after the Columbine high school shooting in Littleton, Colorado, I spoke softly to individual children as they entered our room at 7:45 a.m. "How are you feeling this morning? After art [their specialist time from 8:00 to 8:50] we'll have time to talk about the school shooting. Let's start our day together in our circle."

Our discussion was stimulated by a story from the book, *I Felt Like I Was From Another Planet*. A fourth-grade Vietnam immigrant had been raised according to Chinese culture. Much to her distress, her class was going to perform a Mexican square dance for the school's Cinco de Mayo celebration. She was aghast when it became obvious that she was supposed to touch a boy to do the dance. "My parents always reminded me not to hold hands or have contact with the opposite sex. Girls were to behave properly and not flirt with boys." Questions to my children. . . . What is she feeling? What is she going to do?

The routine of our morning circle was comforting. We were all here. We were safe. Ironically, the morning quote was "Make no judgments where you have no compassion." I asked, "What's compassion?" Children responded. I read from our morning book, *Making the Most of Today.* "What kinds of things are important to you and your friends—your group? Does it matter what people wear, what music they listen to, how they act, what they believe? What happens when someone doesn't fit your picture or follow your rules? Sometimes groups can be cruel to outsiders. They can be quick to gossip, judge, and criticize. Does this sound like your group?" I asked, "Have you ever felt excluded from a group?" The children shared playground incidents and exclusion during a boy scout camping experience. They know the pain of exclusion. I closed our brief time together with the book's thought, "Today I won't judge others," and moved my students off to their art class.

This happened to be a day we were having 12 visitors who had read my first book, *Seeing With Magic Glasses,* in a class at St. Catherine's University. They were coming to observe the classroom I had described. At about 8:15 the visitors began arriving. I greeted them, showed them around, chatted about regular class functions, and explained that our normal routine would be altered today because we needed time, as a group, to process our feelings related to the Columbine School shootings. There was an uncomfortableness on the part of some visitors, a sense of invading my students' privacy, but I believed it would be all right. My students were used to visitors, even if today there were a lot (12 extra people take a lot of space), and even if our topic was sensitive. I asked the visitors to stand behind the counter that divides our room, leaving some breathing room between them and our circle meeting area.

When the children returned, I acknowledged the presence of our visitors. Then, talking very calmly, I asked what they had heard and seen about the shooting. We clarified the story. I had purposefully not brought in the newspaper, which I usually do, to discuss news events. I did not want to further etch pictures in my children's visual memories. I asked for feeling words that related to the tragedy and wrote them on the chalkboard . . . scared, terrified, rageful, tearful. . . . Mike raised his hand, "Could we get the feeling puppets out today?" "That's a good idea Mike, I'll get them." I walked to my storage closet,

Mature empathy and morality are possible only after an individual develops the ability to connect emotions and ideas, to reflect on himself and his actions, and finally to construct an inner world of stable values alongside that of changing experiences.
—Stanley Greenspan (1997), *The Growth of the Mind*, p. 122

past the visitors who were quietly frozen. I collected the puppets and put them into Numbfull's pouch, then returned to our circle. The puppets would help us through this discussion. I was pleased that I had taught the puppets earlier in the year, because now they are an available resource.

First, I reviewed Numbfull, an 18-inch gray stuffed character with a large stomach pocket. "You might be feeling numb like Numbfull and be stuffing your emotions. Did any of you get a stomachache or headache that might be from the shooting news?"

Hands go up. "How did you feel? What feelings do you think might have gotten stuffed?" Responses. "Do you think anyone in Colorado is numb? Who?" Parents are numb. Friends are numb. Teachers are numb.

I took green Tearfull out of Numbfull's pocket. "Who might be tearful today?" The conversation continued. I asked who felt they would like to have Tearfull today, and I passed it to a child. I continued the discussion with blue Fearfull, orange Stressfull, and red Ragefull, passing each to a waiting child. We talked of our own feelings and linked to the possible feelings of the people this tragedy has touched. One student expressed concern for the parents of the boys who did the shooting, a profound thought of empathy from a 10-year-old.

Finally, I brought out our two purple Powerfull puppets. I had purposefully saved them until last. "Sometimes when bad things happen we let our individual power slip away with feeling fear or anger. It's important that you recognize your feelings. It's also important that you keep your own power to be successful in your own life. We are safe. We need to keep our power directed toward good relationships in our classroom and our school. As we continue today, you need to keep your personal power focused on what you need to do to have a successful day. Who would like to start with Powerfull as their companion?"

This circle meeting took about 45 minutes, much longer than our usual meeting at this time of the day. Students shared honestly and listened to each other. They showed empathy for the people in Columbine and for each other. As we got involved in the discussion, the children seemed to forget about the 12

words for the greatest effect. A skilled communicator taps both intrapersonal and interpersonal skills.

- A responsible citizen manages her emotions appropriately. She feels capable of contributing to the community. She respects the diversity of our world and connects with others empathetically. She understands social norms and is willing to work with others to solve problems. These abilities stem from good intrapersonal skills and extend to other people within the interpersonal domain.
- A self-directed adult reflects on his life. He sets goals and makes decisions that are realistic. He manages his life effectively.
- People who contribute to their community exhibit intrapersonal and interpersonal skills. Their self-management skills are on automatic pilot, enabling them to focus attention on issues in our community rather than on themselves. They can organize to solve problems.

All of these competencies depend on intrapersonal and interpersonal intelligences, yet compared to the educational concerns around reading and math, there is little guidance for teachers who seek to facilitate these goals.

Developing Assets

Recently, my district adopted the Search Institute's concept of 40 Developmental Assets. The Institute did extensive research linking behaviors of youths with their self-management strategies. The conclusion, based on 100,000 youths in 213 communities across the United States, was that the youths with the greater number of "assets" had less high-risk behaviors. It makes sense, of course. Those youths who delay gratification, value diversity, take care of their health, and do well in school, are the same young people who avoid alcohol, drugs, and early sexual experiences. The research on the 40 Developmental Assets provides a powerful statement.

As I reflected on the asset principles, I linked the "internal assets" to intrapersonal intelligence and most of the "external

Figure 9.1. 40 Developmental Assets for Elementary-Age Children

 40 Developmental Assets for Elementary-Age Children

Search Institute has identified a framework of 40 developmental assets for children ages 6 to 11 that blends Search Institute's research on developmental assets for 12- to 18-year-olds with the extensive literature in child development. For more information, see *Starting Out Right: Developmental Assets for Children* (published by Search Institute in 1997).

	CATEGORY	ASSET NAME AND DEFINITION
EXTERNAL ASSETS	**Support**	1. **Family support**—Family life provides high levels of love and support. 2. **Positive family communication**—Parent(s) and child communicate positively. Child is willing to seek parent(s) advice and counsel. 3. **Other adult relationships**—Child receives support from nonparent adults. 4. **Caring neighborhood**—Child experiences caring neighbors. 5. **Caring school climate**—School provides a caring, encouraging environment. 6. **Parent involvement in schooling**—Parent(s) are actively involved in helping child succeed in school.
	Empowerment	7. **Community values children**—Children feel that the community values and appreciates children. 8. **Children given useful roles**—Child is included in family decisions and is given useful roles at home and in the community. 9. **Service to others**—Child and parent(s) serve others and the community. 10. **Safety**—Child is safe at home, at school, and in the neighborhood.
	Boundaries & Expectations	11. **Family boundaries**—Family has clear rules and consequences and monitors the child's whereabouts. 12. **School boundaries**—School provides clear rules and consequences. 13. **Neighborhood boundaries**—Neighbors take responsibility for monitoring the child's behavior. 14. **Adult role models**—Parent(s) and other adults model positive, responsible behavior. 15. **Positive peer interactions**—Child plays with children who model responsible behavior. 16. **Expectations for growth**—Adults have realistic expectations of development at this age. Parent(s), caregivers, and other adults encourage child to achieve and develop his or her unique talents.
	Constructive Use of Time	17. **Creative activities**—Child participates in music, arts, or drama three or more hours each week through home and out-of-home activities. 18. **Child programs**—Child spends one hour or more per week in extracurricular school or structured community programs. 19. **Religious community**—Family attends religious programs or services for at least one hour once a week. 20. **Positive, supervised time at home**—Child spends most evenings and weekends at home with parent(s) in predictable and enjoyable routines.
INTERNAL ASSETS	**Commitment to Learning**	21. **Achievement motivation**—Child is motivated to do well in school. 22. **School engagement**—Child is responsive, attentive, and actively engaged in learning. 23. **Homework**—Child does homework when it is assigned. 24. **Bonding to school**—Child cares about her or his school. 25. **Reading for pleasure**—Child and a caring adult read together for at least 30 minutes a day. Child also enjoys reading without an adult's involvement.
	Positive Values	26. **Caring**—Child is encouraged to help other people and to share her or his possessions. 27. **Equality and social justice**—Child begins to show interest in making the community a better place. 28. **Integrity**—Child begins to act on convictions and stand up for her or his beliefs. 29. **Honesty**—Child begins to value honesty and act accordingly. 30. **Responsibility**—Child begins to accept and take personal responsibility for age-appropriate tasks. 31. **Healthy lifestyle and sexual attitudes**—Child begins to value good health habits. Child learns healthy sexual attitudes and beliefs and to respect others.
	Social Competencies	32. **Planning and decision making**—Child learns beginning skills of how to plan ahead and makes decisions at an appropriate developmental level. 33. **Interpersonal competence**—Child interacts with adults and children and can make friends. Child expresses and articulates feelings in appropriate ways and empathizes with others. 34. **Cultural competence**—Child has knowledge of and comfort with people of different cultural/racial/ethnic backgrounds. 35. **Resistance skills**—Child begins to develop the ability to resist negative peer pressure and dangerous situations. 36. **Peaceful conflict resolution**—Child attempts to resolve conflict nonviolently.
	Positive Identity	37. **Personal power**—Child begins to feel he or she has control over "things that happen to me." Child begins to manage life's frustrations and challenges in ways that have positive results for the child and others. 38. **Self-esteem**—Child reports having a high self-esteem. 39. **Sense of purpose**—Child reports that "my life has a purpose." 40. **Positive view of personal future**—Child is optimistic about her or his personal future.

assets" to interpersonal intelligence. The assets point to the same end states as personal intelligence. We want our young people to be attentive to their schoolwork. We want our young people to really care about what they learn. We want them to be honest, responsible, and have empathy for others. We want them to become effective self-managers, planners, and decision makers. We want our young people to feel a sense of personal power and a sense of purpose. These hopes and dreams encompass the personal intelligences.

In my classroom, it's obvious that children with higher parent involvement and children with additional experiences in the arts (music, drama, painting) or neighborhood sports teams are also academic achievers. Usually the children who behave responsibly and treat others with respect achieve academically as well. When children have the developmental assets, they tend to be more successful! Yes! The list of 40 Developmental Assets is wonderful. But . . . the list doesn't help teachers understand how to help children achieve the assets. We know this is what we want for our children, but how do we help children who don't have these qualities develop these qualities?

Curriculum Standards

My district's standards for fifth and sixth grades link to the 40 Developmental Assets. Many of the standards are within health education, an aspect of the curriculum too often neglected because of the demands of other instructional time. Here is a sampling of the Minneapolis standards (Grade Level Expectations, 1998):

- Identify personal values
- Describe positive qualities about oneself
- Identify potential stressors in their lives
- Identify how the body responds to stress
- Identify personal stressors in daily living
- Describe methods of stress management
- Describe respectful/disrespectful behaviors

- Identify actions that are risky or harmful to self or others
- Describe ways to avoid, recognize and respond to negative social influences and pressure to use alcohol, drugs, and tobacco
- Demonstrate refusal and negotiation skills that could be used to protect self and others from violent and/or abusive situations
- Name strategies and skills to attain personal health goals
- Identify peer group's positive and negative influences
- Solve different conflicts using effective communication and mediation
- Describe how perseverance relates to personal goals
- Communicate effectively, resolve conflict peacefully, negotiate successfully
- Manage reactions to insults, discrimination, and escalation of conflicts
- Contribute to effective teamwork
- Identify cooperative and social skills that facilitate working in a group
- Gain tolerance for people of diverse backgrounds
- Describe links between risk factors and responsible behaviors
- Define body language
- Distinguish between verbal and nonverbal communication
- Identify factors that can affect health
- Identify how emotions can affect eating
- Develop goals regarding personal health, food, and fitness
- Make good food selections that reduce the risk of disease

I am comforted knowing these standards are in place in my school district. I am discomforted with the sense that these standards are not receiving enough attention.

Middle Grades Platform

In a 1998 document, "A Platform for Effective Middle Grades Education in the Minneapolis Public Schools," my district articulates its commitment to teaching students management and problem-solving skills. Students are also to learn to set goals and do appropriate self-assessment.

There is a commitment to promote good health because "the education and health of young adolescents are inextricably linked." This includes positive physical and emotional health and character education. There is a commitment to "actively involve students and parents in individual goal setting" with face-to-face communication. There is a commitment to empowering students' relationships with our communities through service learning. The "Platform for Effective Middle Grades Education" acknowledges social/emotional development as a key to successful students in early adolescence. These issues are part of the personal intelligences. And once again, as correct as this position is, basically it leaves the "how to do it" to teacher ingenuity. Whereas I affirm these goals, many teachers seem uncomfortable with how to facilitate such student growth.

It is gratifying to have Eliot Brenner and Peter Salovey provide a firm foundation for understanding what teachers experience daily in the classroom concerning students' emotional regulation. It is disturbing, however, that the development of emotional regulation does not currently have a definable place in the curriculum.
—Patricia Moore Harbour and Jill Stewart, "Educator's Commentary" in Emotional Development and Emotional Intelligence, Peter Salovey and David Sluyter (1997), p. 193

What Employers Want

From yet a different arena, the U.S. Secretary of Labor's Commission on Achieving Necessary Skills (SCANS) identified three foundational skills in answer to the question "What Are Workplace Skills?" I've italicized the descriptors that connect to the personal intelligences.

- Basic skills—reading, writing, speaking, *listening*, and know-

Since early adolescence is a crucial period in establishing a clear self-concept and positive self-esteem, assessment and evaluation should emphasize individual progress rather than comparison with other students. The goal is to help students discover and understand their strengths, weakness, interest, values and personalities. Student self-evaluation is an important means of developing a fair and realistic self-concept.
—The National Middle Schools Association (1998), "A Platform for Effective Middle Grades Education in the Minneapolis Public Schools," p. 3

Milwaukee's Goals

1. Students will project anti-racist, anti-biased attitudes through their participation in a multi-lingual, multi-ethnic, culturally diverse curriculum.

2. Students will participate and gain knowledge in all the arts, developing personal vehicles for self-expression reinforced in an integrated curriculum.

3. Students will demonstrate positive attitudes towards life, living, and learning, through an understanding and respect of self and others.

4. Students will make responsible decisions, solve problems, and think critically.

5. Students will demonstrate responsible citizenship and an understanding of global interdependence.

6. Students will use technological resources capably, actively, and responsibly.

7. Students will think logically and abstractly, applying mathematical and scientific principles of inquiry to solve problems, create new solutions, and communicate new ideas and relationships to real world experiences.

8. Students will communicate knowledge, ideas, thoughts, feelings, concepts, opinions, and needs effectively and creatively using varied modes of expression.

9. Students will learn strategies to cope with the challenges of daily living and will establish practices which promote health, fitness, and safety.

10. Students will set short- and long-term goals, will develop an awareness of career opportunities and will be motivated to actualize their potential.

Milwaukee's 10 Teaching and Learning Goals were published in the fall 1998 issue of the *Rethinking Schools* newspaper.

ing arithmetic and mathematical concepts
- Thinking skills—*reasoning, making decisions, thinking creatively, solving problems,* seeing things in the mind's eye, and *knowing how to learn*

- Personal qualities—*responsibility, self-esteem, sociability, self-management, integrity, and honesty* (Whetzel, 1992)

It is noteworthy that 12 of the 17 items relate to the personal intelligences.

Implications of Neurobiology

Finally, writing in *Emotional Development and Emotional Intelligence,* Mark Greenberg and Jennie Snell from the Department of Psychology, University of Washington, list five "Implications of the Neurobiology of Emotion for Education":

1. The nature and quality of teacher-child and peer-peer social and academic interactions impacts brain development, attention, and learning. During development the nature of social and educational interactions plays an active r.ole in shaping the brain. Of special importance is how education and social experience create healthy neural networks between the frontal lobes and the subcortical emotion centers (primarily the amygdala).

2. Education can be considered to be a critical influence on strengthening neocortical control and self-awareness. Of particular importance is the manner in which teachers promote cognitive and interpersonal decision making and problem solving in the classroom.

3. The strengthening of frontal lobe capacities (maintenance of attention, social problem-solving skills, frustration tolerance, and the management of negative and positive affect) is critical to academic, social, and personal outcomes.

4. Helping children develop awareness of emotional processes (both in themselves and in others), applying verbal labels to emotions, and encouraging perspective taking and empathic identification with others are the first steps in developing these frontal lobe functions of interper-

> *People with particularly strong intrapersonal intelligence are prized in the business world because they can make optimal use of their talents, especially under rapidly changing conditions, and they know best how to mesh their talents with those of their coworkers.*
>
> —Howard Gardner (1999b), *Intelligence Reframed,* p. 200

sonal awareness and self-control. Children who show the most impulsive and aggressive behavior have the least access to verbalizing and discussing their emotions.

5. Attending patiently to children's emotions and their effects as a central part of classroom processes will lead to improved personal and academic outcomes. Teaching healthy strategies for coping with, communicating about, and managing emotions assists children in maintaining attention and focus during academic and interpersonal learning contexts. (Greenberg & Snella, 1997, pp. 112-113)

From diverse sources, there is a recognition of the need to address the development of intrapersonal and interpersonal intelligences.

RESOURCES

There is a wide range of materials to support teaching to personal intelligences. Some materials, such as The New City School's manual, *Succeeding With Multiple Intelligences: Teaching Through the Personal Intell igences,* provide suggestions for lessons at different grade levels. Other materials, represented by the Responsive Classroom, offer insights into classroom management strategies that facilitate the development of children's personal intelligences. Additional materials are available from such sources as the Committee for Children, the Association for Supervision and Curriculum Development (ASCD), the Collaborative for the Advancement of Social and Emotional Learning (CASEL), the New Haven Public Schools, the Resolving Conflict Creatively Program, and others.

> *Ironically, social and emotional skills, attitudes, and values have been embraced most enthusiastically in the boardrooms of corporate America. Moreover, businesses of all sizes have come to realize that productivity depends on a work force that is socially and emotionally competent.*
> —Maurice Elias et al. (1997),
> *Promoting Social and Emotional Learning, p. 6*

Succeeding With Multiple Intelligences

Succeeding With Multiple Intelligences[1] is the second multiple intelligences book published by an independent school in St. Louis, Missouri. In the introduction they write, "More and more, as we work with MI we see that the personal intelligences are the most important intelligences." I would certainly agree.

The book has three sections: Intrapersonal, Interpersonal, and Reaching Out With MI. Individual chapters provide teacher-developed lessons in Bodily-Kinesthetic, Linguistic, Logical-Mathematical, Musical, and Spatial Intelligences. Each lesson has clearly stated learner outcomes, materials needed, procedures, and assessment suggestions. As teachers experience using these lessons, I believe they would begin to transfer the ideas to other experiences within their own class-rooms. The resource book has excellent lists of activities that support Intrapersonal and Interpersonal Intelligences.

The last section discusses personal intelligence issues in relation to a wide variety of important issues beyond direct classroom activities—authentic assessments, portfolios, par-ents as partners, teacher growth, and developmental issues. These are valuable discussions written by practicing teachers. This is an excellent resource for teachers.

The Responsive Classroom

The Responsive Classroom comes from the Northeast Foundation for Children, a nonprofit educational organization in Massachusetts. Last year, my school began a three-year commitment for professional growth focused on the Responsive Classroom and the arts. We believe this combination will lead to greater academic achieve-ment for our K through 8 stu-dents. Movement, music, visual arts, and drama stimulate vast regions of the brain. Children's ability to attend to details is significantly enhanced by teaching drawing skills. The arts, along with the personal intelligences, dominate the eight

To argue for the importance of emotion and attention in cognition doesn't suggest that reason and logic are unimportant. Reason and logic consciously move us toward an intelligent, learned response that's typically our first choice when we confront the problem again. Our brain thus developed two separate but integrated systems, and the transcendent movement patterns that characterize the arts often provide the integration between emotion/attention and reason/logic. Only the mindless would suggest that education can function with one system but not the other. Only the unimaginative would suggest that both systems must be judged by the same criteria of economy, efficiency, and objective measurability. This discussion of the arts began with the importance of motion, and it ends with the importance of emotion. Both are central to the arts and to life. They're two inseparable sides of a very valuable biological coin that each generation must invest in its young. School arts programs are a worthy investment of that coin.
—Robert Sylwester (1998), "Art for the Brain's Sake," *Educational Leadership*, p. 35

It would be wonderful if each growing individual had some opportunity to create in an art form. There is no substitute for drawing a portrait or a still life, composing a song or a sonnet, choreographing and performing a dance. Education early in life ought to provide such opportunities to think and perform in an artistic medium.
—Howard Gardner (1999a), *The Disciplined Mind,* p. 151

forms of intelligence. Arts are important vehicles for expressing ideas of the naturalist, logical-mathematics, and linguistic intelligence.

Our school's project with The Responsive Classroom is directly related to the intrapersonal and interpersonal intelligences. One of the components of The Responsive Classroom is the morning meeting. Throughout the school as morning meetings begin, we greet each other, listen to one another, share, and ask questions. In the first- through fourth-grade classrooms, a simple greeting is passed around the circle: "Good morning, how are you, _____ (person's name)?"

In September, when we don't know each other's names well, I begin this way. Later, I increase the skill level of our greeting process. Instead of greeting the person next to us, we greet someone across the circle, alternating boy/girl. Students' eye contact follows the individual speaking. In a few weeks, I expand the skills by modeling a brief reflective question that children ask of each other. For example, to review emotional vocabulary, I'll ask, "Since we were together yesterday I've felt proud that I accomplished another chapter in the book I'm writing, but frustrated when I reread it because I need to rearrange a number of sentences. What feelings have you had since yesterday, Sydney?" Another day, the reading from our morning book stimulated this morning exchange. "The quote today is from Elbert Hubbard: 'The greatest mistake you can make in this life is to be continually fearing you will make one.' I made a mistake when I forgot my friend's birthday, and she felt bad. When did you make a mistake, Lee?" Lee makes his own statement, then asks the question of someone else. Children need to pay attention to remember

Teachers have long known and researchers are now confirming that social skills are not just something to be taught so that children behave well enough to get on with the real business of schooling. Rather, they are inextricably intertwined with cognitive growth and intellectual progress. A person who can listen well, who can frame a good question and has the assertiveness to pose it, who can examine a situation from a number of perspectives will be a strong learner. All those skills—skills essential to academic achievement—must be modeled, experienced, practiced, extended and refined in the context of social interaction.
—Roxann Kriete (1999), *The Morning Meeting Book,* p. 9

The Seven Tenets of The Responsive Classroom Approach

1. The social curriculum is as important as the academic curriculum.

2. How children learn is as important as what children learn.

3. The greatest cognitive growth occurs through social interaction.

4. There is a set of social skills that children need to learn and practice in order to be successful. They form the acronym CARES—Cooperation, Assertion, Responsibility, Empathy, Self-Control.

5. Educators must know children individually, culturally, and developmentally.

6. All parents want what's best for their children and educators must work with parents as partners.

7. The principles of The Responsive Classroom must be practiced by educators in their interactions with each other, with the children, and with the parents.

SOURCE: Northeast Foundation for Children, 71 Montague City Road, Greenfield, MA 01301. Phone: 1-800-360-6332; Reprinted with permission. www.responsiveclassroom.org

who has had a chance to share and who still needs to be called on. The process is very respectful. Everyone has a chance to speak and is listened to as eye contact shifts from one to another.

Part of our morning meeting is student sharing. Each morning, children who want to share sit on the bench in our circle. The child shares only a sentence or two, not paragraphs, and then says, "Questions or comments, please." This process significantly improves student listening and interaction. Kaelyn, for instance, just came back from a trip. She's brought some rocks she found. She begins, "I went on a trip with my parents, and I found these rocks. Questions and comments, please." Kaelyn has said enough to pique the interest of the other children and the discussion of rocks becomes a two-way street, not a monologue. This Responsive Classroom technique has been a nice improvement in our sharing time.

Other components of The Responsive Classroom include creating classroom expectations together, a "guided discovery" that helps students think about learning materials and classroom routines, academic choice, mutual communication with parents, and strategies of classroom organization. Each of these fosters elements of personal intelligences. The Northeast Foundation for Children is a rich resource for materials relating to The Responsive Classroom.

Second Step

Second Step,[2] created by Committee for Children, has a training component and specific social-skills materials for preschool through 9th grade. Kits include poster-size pictures with stories to discuss and role-play. There are accompanying videos, parent materials, and a teacher's guide. Topics include problem solving, impulse control, dealing with anger, developing empathy, and more. If your school is looking for a total package, these materials might be a good choice for you. Second Step is a social-skills program; developing children's personal intelligences is broader than social skills. The program has a teacher-training component.

ASCD and CASEL

A joint project between the Association for Supervision and Curriculum Development (ASCD) and the Collaborative for the Advancement of Social and Emotional Learning (CASEL), a broad-based collaborative of university people across the United States, produced *Promoting Social and Emotional Learning: Guidelines for Educators*. The web site, www.casel. org, is an excellent site for continual discussion of social-emotional learning, and it provides information on new resources. The book provides background on the research relating to social and emotional education. It provides basic principles of social-emotional learning (SEL), resources, and examples of schools with extensive programming. Because it is published

New Haven's Curriculum

K-3rd grade	35-55 lessons using Project Charlie and Building Blocks (AIDS)
4th-5th	25 lessons using Second Step, Human Sexuality, Substance Use
6th	45 lessons using Social Problem Solving, Substance Use Prevention, Human Growth, AIDS and Teen Pregnancy Prevention
7th	25 lessons on You and Your Relationships
8th	20 lessons in math on Making the Most of School, 10 in PE on choices
9th	47-57 lessons on decision making (Crossroads), substance use, AIDS and violence prevention (Protecting Oneself and Others)
10th	47 lessons on Violence Prevention, Conflict Resolution, and Strengthening Relationships with Family and Friends
11th	37 lessons integrated in U.S. History, (A World of Difference and Substance Use Prevention) and 3 in English (HIV/AIDS education)
12th	16 lessons in their senior guidance class (Transition Skills for Life), and 5-10 in English (Substance use prevention and HIV/AIDS).

SOURCE: Reprinted from *Social Development Curriculum*, New Haven Public Schools, with permission.

by ASCD, it is a good place to start as you encourage your school to develop a comprehensive program.

New Haven Public Schools

The New Haven district is discussed extensively in *Promoting Social and Emotional Learning*.[3] In 1987, the superintendent formed a task force to assess high-risk behaviors in

Would a 45-minute auditorium program be an appropriate way to teach math? Hardly. Neither does it work for social skills. Social skills should be taught in the same way as academic skills.
—Karol DeFalco,
"Educator's Commentary,"
in *Emotional Development and Emotional Intelligence*, Peter Salovey and David Sluyter (1997), p. 34

students that led to low school achievement. The result of the study was a district-wide Department of Social Development, which coordinates all prevention and health promotion activities. Using many sources of commercially available curriculum, New Haven implemented a K-through-12 curriculum. Some grades include specific Life Skills classes. In other grades, the lessons are integrated with subject areas. Every grade has designated topics and instructional materials. Teachers are given 25 to 50 hours of inservice support, depending on the lessons they are expected to teach.

Beginning in kindergarten, students work on self-awareness and decision making. In fourth and fifth grades the emphasis is on impulse control, anger management, and empathy. Middle school students learn stress management, problem identification, goal setting, planning, solution generating, and peer pressure resistance skills. High schoolers focus on relationships and decisions.

The New Haven preventive curriculum is comprehensive because research indicates piecemeal programs are not successful. In a survey of more than 200 New Haven teachers, more than 95% thought the curriculum addresses important issues for their children. About 80% of the teachers felt the program improved communication with their students. The director of the program counters a common question—whether school time should be used for teaching personal social/emotional skills—with a math analogy. Why do we teach division, for example . . . to have the skill when we need it in everyday life. Math is so important it is taught sequentially, every day. Social skills are just as important.

Another program that is highly respected in the educational literature is the Resolving Conflict Creatively Program.[4] Many of the elementary and middle schools using this program are in the New York City/New Jersey area. The curriculum focuses on six themes: cooperation, caring communication, expression of feelings, appreciation of diversity, responsible decision making, and conflict resolution. There is a large component of training for teachers, administrators, and parents.

Additional Teacher Resources

I Felt Like I Was From Another Planet, by Norine Dresser, is a collection of short stories relating to embarrassing experiences due to cultural misunderstandings. The stories are from Asian and Latino students writing in a class at a California State University. In one story, a Vietnamese girl shows concern for an African girl wearing a white headband, because in Vietnam that headband would represent a death in the family. In another story, a recent refugee from Vietnam is thrilled with her new clothes and proudly wears them to school the first day, only to find out they are pajamas.

I have read the stories aloud and simply discussed them to raise students' sense of empathy. I have read a story, then used the follow-up activities, including having the children suggest the feelings of each different character in the story. The stories have excellent potential to stimulate children's writing about their own embarrassing experiences.

Starting Small and the "Teaching Tolerance" magazine are produced by the Southern Poverty Law Center.[5] *Starting Small* is meant for teachers of preschool and primary, but I found it full of transferable ideas for my classroom. The magazine always has stories that have the potential for reading aloud to children. Both are free to teachers, but then you'll be on their mailing lists for donations.

Articles in *Starting Small* introduced me to the "colors of people" tempera paints. I begin by asking the children, "What colors are people?" Black, white . . . then I show a bottle of cosmetic foundation, "Sometimes women wear foundation to smooth the color of their face. The tone has to be just right or it looks funny. This week when you draw your hand we're going to mix the exact color of your hand. Take a small brush and try different combinations until it really is your color. On the bottom of your drawing describe which of the colors you used and about how much." The children's drawings turned out wonderful, and we posted them on our hallway bulletin board. Finally, we discussed why we use terms like black and white, and came to understand that we are a wide range of hues, much richer than black and white.

Boulden Publishing has a series of coloring books for children in K through second grade, but I've used them with hurting

New Haven Social Development Curriculum Scope for K-12

Skills of Self-Management:
- Self-monitoring
- Self-control
- Stress management
- Persistence
- Emotion-focused coping
- Self-reward

Skills of Problem Solving and Decision Making:
- Problem recognition
- Feelings awareness
- Perspective taking
- Realistic and adaptive goal setting
- Awareness of adaptive response strategies
- Consequential thinking
- Decision making
- Planning
- Behavior enactment

Skills of Communication:
- Understanding nonverbal communication
- Sending messages
- Receiving messages
- Matching communication to the situation

Attitudes and Values About Self:
- Self-respect
- Feeling capable
- Honesty
- Sense of responsibility
- Willingness to grow
- Self-acceptance

**New Haven Social Development
Curriculum Scope for K-12** *(continued)*

Attitudes and Values About Others:
- Awareness of social norms and values (peers, family, community, society)
- Accepting individual differences
- Respecting human dignity
- Having concern or compassion for others
- Valuing cooperation with others
- Motivation to solve interpersonal problems
- Motivation to contribute

Attitudes and Values About Tasks:
- Willingness to work hard
- Motivation to solve practical problems
- Motivation to solve academic problems
- Recognition of the importance of education
- Respect for property

SOURCE: Elias et al. (1997). *Promoting Social and Emotional Learning* (p. 4). Reprinted with permission of Roger Weissburg.

fifth and sixth graders. I have used these titles: *Divorce Happens, Playground Push-Around, Goodbye Forever,* and *Life With One Parent.*[6]

BullyProof is a publication of The Wellesley College Center for Research on Women and the NEA Professional Library. It is a spiral-bound teacher's guide targeted for fourth through fifth grades. Included are activities, reproducible handouts, discussion ideas, and background information. One lesson was very successful in my classroom. I asked my students to write in columns, "What does a bully . . . sound like? act like? feel like?" Every child wrote numerous characteristics for each category. We discussed experiences. Then I asked, "What does a friend sound like, act like, and feel like?" It was a powerful process.[7]

Free Spirit Publishing is a wonderful source of many materials supporting the development of Interpersonal and Intrapersonal Intelligence. The company's recent book, *The Bully Free Classroom,* is an outstanding resource. Thirty-four reproducible pages provide teachers with instant, well-designed activities relating to the personal intelligences. The company's focus is publishing self-help materials for kids and books that empower students. I use two books by Trevor Romain, *Bullies Are a Pain in the Brain* and *Cliques, Phonies & Other Baloney,* for discussion of issues. I use *What Do You Stand For? A Kid's Guide to Building Character* and *Fighting Invisible Tigers: A Stress Management Guide for Teens* as topic starters during themes. Children in my room thoroughly enjoy taking the questionnaires in *Psychology for Kids,* and we use *Making the Most of Today* during our morning meeting. Two books travel home with kids often—*Perfectionism: What's Bad About Being Too Good* and *Bringing Up Parents: The Teenager's Handbook.* This is a catalog I strongly recommend.[8]

Finally, the line drawings of emotions and other good information come from Wellness Reproductions & Publishing, Inc.[9]

New materials are being published each year that provide teachers with ideas and guidance. Teaching personal intelligences can become a priority integrated within other curriculum.

NOTES

1. *Succeeding With Multiple Intelligences: Teaching Through the Personal Intelligences,* ($34), from The New City School, 5209 Waterman Avenue, St. Louis, MO 63108. Phone: 314-361-6411; FAX 314-361-1499.

2. Second Step, Committee for Children, 2203 Airport Way South, Suite 500, Seattle, WA 98134. Web site: www.cfchildren.org

3. Social Development Department, Hillhouse, 480 Sherman Parkway, New Haven, CT 06511. FAX: 203-946-7448.

4. Director Linda Lantieri, Resolving Conflict Creatively Program, 163 Third Avenue, #103. New York, NY 10003. Phone: 212-387-0225; Web site: http://eric-web.tc.columbia.edu/directories/anti-bias/rccpnatl.html

5. 400 Washington Ave., Montgomery, AL 36104; Web site: www.splcenter.org

6. Boulden Publishing, P.O. Box 1186, Weavervill, CA 96093. Phone: 800-238-8433.

7. Center for Research on Women, Publications Department, Wellesley College, 106 Central St., Wellesley, MA 02181. Phone: 617-283-2500.

8. Free Spirit Publishing, Inc., 400 First Avenue North, Suite 616, Minneapolis, MN 55401-1724. Phone: 800-735-7323; Web site: www.freespirit.com

9. Wellness Reproductions & Publishing, Inc., 23945 Mercantile Road, Suite K3, Beachwood, OH 44122-5924. Phone: 800-669-9208; Web site: www.wellness-resources.com

End Points

Adaptation to the social environment of school calls upon
interpersonal intelligence, while having a sense of oneself as
a learner, with particular strengths, weaknesses, and
stylistic features, draws upon intrapersonal intelligence.

—Howard Gardner (1993, *Multiple Intelligences,* p. 123)

In this book I have detailed the critical importance of
Intrapersonal and Interpersonal Intelligences as the foundation for learning. This includes understanding cause and effect
in order to make good choices. It includes internal self-talk,
which evaluates the potential outcomes of actions. Personal intelligence includes understanding one's strengths and admit-
ting one's weaknesses. It includes self-management—of
thoughts, food, sleep, and exercise. It acknowledges the body-
brain system as one system, respected as an integral whole, im-
pacting learning and thinking.

Children who have poor skills in the Intrapersonal and Interpersonal Intelligences are more difficult to educate. These
children haven't learned the basics of emotional control. They
have more difficulty identifying their anger before they reflexively act out. They are impulsive. They need time to practice,
and practice, and practice using words, such as "I" statements,
to express their emotions appropriately. These children need

Daniel Goleman ends his book, *Emotional Intelligence* (1998), with these three paragraphs:

"One reason they (teens) are so poor at this basic life skill (of avoiding disputes), of course, is that as a society we have not bothered to make sure every child is taught the essentials of handling anger or resolving conflicts positively—nor have we bothered to teach empathy, impulse control, or any of the other fundamentals of emotional competence. By leaving the emotional lessons children learn to chance, we risk largely wasting the window of opportunity presented by the slow maturation of the brain to help children cultivate a healthy emotional repertoire.

"Despite high interest in emotional literacy among some educators, these courses are as yet rare; most teachers, principals, and parents simply do not know they exist. The best models are largely outside the education mainstream, in a handful of private schools and a few hundred public schools. Of course no program, including this one, is an answer to every problem. But given the crisis we find ourselves and our children facing, and given the quantum of hope held out by courses in emotional literacy, we must ask ourselves: Shouldn't we be teaching these most essential skills for life to every child—now more than ever?

"And if not now, when?" (p. 287)

to learn to breathe deeply and soothe themselves. Over and over, children need to remember to "get into their hearts" before dealing with their interpersonal problems.

Children who have difficulty dealing with interpersonal problems are often the same children who do not notice nonverbals. We must not assume children have this tacitly learned ability. We must teach it explicitly. We must be cognizant of the different nonverbal cultural patterns in children's homes, and we must purposely bring such nonverbal patterns to children's attention.

Emotions drive attention. Children with attention problems have much more difficulty learning academic content. Focused attention is a complex skill. Some children have learned attention skills before entering school, others have not. Children with ADD have significant difficulty focusing attention, but so do many other children, particularly if they've experienced a strong diet of TV and less family talk.

Internal self-talk is critical for self-management. Children with little internal talk often seem bewildered by the world. They have no internal voice to process the external stimuli they are experiencing. They have no internal thought process, such as "This is what's happening. I remember when something like this happened. I think I'd better do this . . ." At a beginning level, internal thought connects cause and potential effect. At more advanced levels, internal talk is the vehicle for making plans, evaluating progress, and reflecting on the next steps to achieve a goal. A basic understanding of our brains makes it evident that we need to link to children's prior knowledge before teaching new ideas. Children without internal talk need even more teacher talk to link to their prior knowledge. Making choices strengthens children's internal talk. . . . "What should I do now? How should I begin . . .?" Adults must model this thought process for children.

Children, when not linking cause and effect, do not understand that what they put into their bodies—balanced nutrition or sugary taste-goods—makes a difference in their body-brain functions. They often haven't internalized the need for regular, appropriate exercise to keep their brains nourished with oxygen, water, and nutrients.

The ancient wisdom, "Know thyself," makes sense to individuals with strong intrapersonal intelligence. This inner knowledge includes emotions and reactions. It includes knowing how to optimally manage one's body-brain system; it also includes knowing strengths and weaknesses. It includes knowing which one of the multiple intelligences is your natural inclination. It includes knowing how you face the world—introverted or extraverted. It is understanding your preferences as a morning person or night person, a high-light person or low light. It is knowing yourself in the many realms that affect you. People who know themselves are able to accept the diversity of other people's styles: "I'm a morning person; my daughter is a night person. It's not a question of which is right or wrong."

Understanding ourselves is a prerequisite for mature empathy. As children grow, teachers need to use daily events, the news, and good literature to ask children, "How would you feel in this situation?" Like every learned skill, empathy should be explored and practiced, so it will be a usable skill when needed.

A sense of "how the other person feels" is important as children learn to collaborate on products and processes. You have to know how you think and feel, and then be willing to listen (not just hear) to another person's feelings and ideas. The act of negotiation within cooperative groups represents a sophisticated collection of skills. Children who have good intrapersonal skills have the foundational skills to interact successfully with other people. These skills often determine the success of adults in their jobs. A caring classroom environment is absolutely necessary for teaching the personal intelligences to all of our children.

My classroom is not different from other classrooms. I teach reading and math, social studies and science. I teach in a public school with all the standard expectations of my state. The source of my joys and passion for teaching is not that my children master the state standards. My joy is watching children develop their personal intelligences. Thus, I interweave the curriculum with rich opportunities for children to participate fully in decision making and self-management. Each of us, as teachers, has the opportunity to interweave the personal intelligences throughout our curriculum. Teachers of social studies can easily integrate personal themes into their assignments by asking students to reflect on other times and lives compared to their own. Language arts teachers can select readings related to personal growth issues, and assign reflective writing topics. Science and math teachers can foster the personal intelligences by asking students to reflect on their thoughts. They can provide opportunities for making choices and for working in groups to produce materials to teach each other. All teachers need to reflect on the symbolic messages behind their choice of particular assignments.

> With knowledge changing so rapidly, students must become able—eager—to assume responsibility for their learning. To the extent that students can craft their own goals, keep track of their own accomplishments, reflect on their own thinking and learning—where it has improved, where it continues to fall short—they become partners in their own education. Even more crucially, once formal schooling has concluded, it should have become second nature for adults to keep on learning—sometimes alone, sometimes in groups—for as long as they choose; indeed, one hopes, for the rest of their lives.
> —Howard Gardner (1999a), *The Disciplined Mind*, p. 135

Children are always creating new habits. Shall I provide experiences that prepare them for their future as thoughtful citizens? How can I do less? Information will change, but the integrity of the individual is a lifetime value.

Teaching the personal intelligences is not an extra. Intrapersonal and interpersonal intelligences represent the core of a person, the foundation for academic excellence, and the wisdom necessary for our democracy.

RESOURCE
A

Books Connecting
to Personal Intelligences

Over many years, I have collected books to use with students for developing the personal intelligences. Recently I found a wonderful resource, *The Bookfinder,* Vol. 5, which makes it significantly easier to find just the right book for a specific need. It is an annotated list of books, appropriate for ages 2 to 18, published between 1987 and 1990, and it addresses students' emotional needs and problems. Topics include self-acceptance, school problems, issues of death and mourning, honesty, human differences, and much more. It is an outstanding resource. Here is the list of books I currently have on my shelves that address the personal intelligences.

Book List

Boyd, Candy Dawson. (1987). *Charlie Pippin.* New York: Puffin Books. Charlie is an enterprising 11-year-old black girl who gets in trouble at school and then with her Vietnam-vet father as she joins the "War and Peace" committee. This chapter book leads to discussions about family issues and growing up.

Bunting, Eve. (1991). *Fly Away Home.* New York: Clarion Books. In this picture book, a 5-year-old boy tells how he and his homeless dad live in the airport while the dad is trying to save enough to get an apartment.

Burgess, Barbara Hood. (1994). *The Fred Field.* New York: Bantam Doubleday. A friend (Fred) is murdered in a poor inner-city drug house. The house is torn down, and a neighbor boy creates a ball field in commemoration of Fred.

Buscaglia, Leo. (1982). *The Fall of Freddie the Leaf.* New York: Holt, Rinehart & Winston. A read-aloud book about life and death as the leaves of a tree talk about their experience from their spring birth to their autumn death.

Clark, Margaret Goff. (1980). *Freedom Crossing.* New York: Scholastic. This chapter book tells of a white girl named Laura who discovers that her brother and father are breaking the law by helping runaway slaves. Then she meets 12-year-old Martin, who would rather die than go back into slavery.

Coles, Robert. (1995). *Ruby Bridges.* New York: Scholastic. The poignantly true story of Ruby, the 6-year-old black child who integrated a New Orleans school in 1960. She withstood the hate and changed the system.

Creech, Sharon. (1994). *Walk Two Moons.* New York: HarperCollins. Thirteen-year-old Sal searches for her mother who left home suddenly. Issues of death, grandparents, and friendship.

Davidson, Margaret. (1988). *Jackie Robinson, Bravest Man in Baseball.* New York: Bantam Doubleday. He endured the racism of the United States in the 1940s and broke the color barrier in major league baseball.

Dresser, Norine. (1994). *I Felt Like I Was From Another Planet.* New York: Addison-Wesley. Fifteen personal stories written by students from cultural backgrounds different from mainstream America. Excellent guide for further discussion and writing activities.

Drucker, Malka and Michael Halperin. (1993). *Jacob's Rescue: A Holocaust Story.* New York: Bantam Doubleday. In this chapter book, Jewish Jacob is slipped out of the ghetto to live in hiding with the Rosen family. Powerful.

Elwin, Rosamund and Michele Paulse. (1990). *Asha's Mums.* Toronto, Ontario: Women's Press. A picture book about a primary girl living with two mothers and dealing with school issues.

Estes, Eleanor. (1973). *The Hundred Dresses.* New York: Scholastic. A classic story of the poor girl on the "outs" and her artistic talents, unappreciated until too late. Important ideas about acceptance of others.

Gehret, Jeanne. (1992). *I'm Somebody Too.* Fairport, NY: Verbal Images Press. In this chapter book, Emily's brother is diagnosed with ADD, and all the family's attention is on him. Emily deals with feeling left out and angry.

Gordon, Sheila. (1997). *Waiting for the Rain.* New York: Bantam Doubleday. A black boy and a white boy grow up as friends in South Africa but end up with very different experiences as the apartheid system begins to change.

Greer, Colin and Herbert Kohn, Eds. (1995). *A Call to Character.* New York: HarperCollins. A collection of stories, plays, poems, and excerpts to be read to children on themes of personal character, such as empathy, honesty, fairness, and responsibility. I find this to be an important resource to have at my fingertips. It has top authors and over 200 entries.

Hansen, Joyce. (1997). *I Thought My Soul Would Rise and Fly.* New York: Scholastic. The poignant diary of a slave girl, months after the Civil War is over. She wonders about her fate and the meaning of the changes about her. Important insights into the confusion of the time.

Heron, Ann and Meredith Maran. (1991). *How Would You Feel If Your Dad Was Gay?* Boston: Alyson Publications. An Afro-American brother and sister deal with classmates calling their father "a faggot." The book models healing discussions regarding different kinds of families.

Ho, Minfong. (1997). *The Clay Marble and Related Readings.* Evanston, IL: McDougal Littell. This chapter book is a story of families fleeing their homelands in Cambodia, hoping to reach safety in the refugee camps on the Thailand border. The author poignantly pictures relationships amidst fear, hunger, and danger. Children respond with empathy to this historical fiction.

Holman, Felice. (1974). *Slake's Limbo.* New York: Dell Publishing. A 13-year-old's life is so bad that he decides to live in New York City's subway system. Despair, ingenuity, survival, fear, poverty, and struggle are topics for discussion as I use this story in a book group.

Klein, Norma. (1974). *Confessions of an Only Child.* New York: Dell Publishing. A chapter book about an only child not appreciating the arrival of a new brother. Dealing well with feelings within a family.

Lewis, Barbara. (1998). *What Do You Stand For? A Kid's Guide to Building Character.* Minneapolis: Free Spirit Publishing. Stories of real young people today, along with suggestions for activities and other books.

Lowery, Linda. (1995). *Somebody Somewhere Knows My Name.* Minneapolis: Carolrhoda Books. Two children are abandoned and learn to cope in a shelter for children.

Maruki, Toshi. (1980). *Hiroshima No Pika.* New York: Lothrop, Lee & Shepard Books. This picture book dramatically relays the experience of a little girl when the bomb hit Hiroshima, Japan, on August 6, 1944, 8:15 a.m.

Miles, Miska. (1971). *Annie and the Old One.* Boston: Little, Brown. This picture book enables conversation about the relationship between a child and grandparent about to die. You can sense the quiet rhythm of life on the southwestern desert, and the ways of the Native People.

Millman, Dan. (1991). *Secret of the Peaceful Warrior.* Tiburon, CA: Starseed Press. I use this important picture book to prompt discussions about turning a bully into a friend. Danny gains confidence in himself as an elder teaches him both strength and "bending in the wind."

Mochizuki, Ken. (1993). *Baseball Saved Us.* New York: Lee & Low Books. This picture book tells the story of Japanese families in American desert internment camps during World War II. Playing baseball helped give their lives some sense of order.

O'Conner, Jim. (1991). *Roberto Clemente, All-Star Hero.* New York: Bantam Doubleday. Escaping from poverty in Puerto Rico and dealing with the racism of the United States in the 1960s, Roberto shows his personal greatness.

O'Dell, Scott. (1970). *Sing Down the Moon*. New York: Bantam. This takes place between 1863 and 1865, when Kit Carson captured the Navahos and took them to Fort Sumner, shattering their original ways of living.

O'Dell, Scott and Elizabeth Hall. (1992). *Thunder Rolling in the Mountains*. New York: Bantam. A story of the Nez Perce, beginning in 1877 when they encounter white people. Eventually they surrender and are taken to reservation lands in the Oklahoma area.

Oppenheim, Joanne. (1979). *Sequoyah: Cherokee Hero*. Mahwah, NJ: Troll Associates. I use this book to foster discussions on what it means to strive toward your goals even if others don't understand or approve of you.

Paterson, Katherine. (1991). *Lyddie*. New York: Penguin. The story of a young girl working six days a week in a weaving factory during the days before child-labor laws. She decides she must stand up for the rights of all the workers.

Paterson, Katherine. (1988). *Park's Quest*. New York: Trumpet Club. Park's father died in Vietnam, and his mother won't even speak about his father. Twelve-year-old Park eventually figures out he has a Vietnamese half-sister. This book leads to discussions of family secrets, the relationship between mothers and sons, and the relationship between the boy and his grandfather, who is impaired by a stroke.

Phelps, Ethel Johnston, Ed. (1978). *Tatterhood and Other Tales*. New York: Feminist Press. A collection of tales from a number of countries where strong girls are the important main characters.

Pinkney, Andrea. (1995). *Hold Fast to Dreams*. New York: Hyperion Books. A fiction, chapter book about a seventh-grade black girl moving into a white suburb. Issues of figuring out how to be yourself in a very different setting.

Polacco, Patricia. (1998). *Thank You, Mr. Falker*. New York: Philomel Books. This autobiographical picture book is full of feeling, telling the story of a fifth grader struggling to learn to read and of the real teacher who helps her.

Richter, Conrad. (1953). *The Light in the Forest*. New York: Bantam. A white boy adopted by the Lenni Lenape Indians when he was four years old is forcibly returned to his white family at age twelve. The story weaves issues of family, adoption, differing customs, and a sense of identity.

Sebestyen, Ouida. (1979). *Words By Heart*. New York: Bantam. When black Lena shows her excellent Bible-quoting skills she just wants to make her father proud. Instead, she is perceived as a threat, and her family is the target of violence.

Seuss, Dr. (1984). *The Butter Battle Book*. New York: Random House. A lively story about the "right" way to do things, and the potential of escalating violence.

Seuss, Dr. (1989). *The Sneetches and Other Stories*. New York: Random House. The Star-Belly Sneetches think they're better than the other Sneetches, but due to the Fix-it-up Chappie, nobody can figure out who is who.

Sharpe, Susan. (1993). *Spirit Quest*. New York: Puffin Books. Aaron goes to the Quileute Indian Reservation with his parents and develops a friendship with a Quileute boy. Their "spirit quest" camping experience takes unexpected courage. The story provides an opportunity to discuss images of Native Americans, friendship building, taking risks, getting in over your head, and finding the courage to do what needs to be done.

Shea, Pegi Deitz. (1995). *The Whispering Cloth*. Honesdale, PA: Boyds Mills Press. This picture book takes place in a refugee camp in Thailand. It is a little girl's life story of the war, her dead parents, and her dreams of leaving the camp inside an airplane all stitched into the traditional Hmong cloth.

Shreve, Susan. (1991). *The Gift of the Girl Who Couldn't Hear*. New York: Beech Tree. Two seventh-grade girls, one deaf, are each auditioning for a musical. They learn about friendship and helping each other.

Silverstein, Shel. (1986). *The Giving Tree*. New York: HarperCollins. A simple picture book of a tree's relationship with a boy over his lifetime. Useful for discussing relationships.

Slote, Alfred. (1982). *Clone Catcher*. New York: J.B. Lippincott. A detective tries to find a runaway clone needed to provide an organ transplant. Brings up lots of issues about life and cloning humans.

Smith, Doris Buchanan. (1973). *A Taste of Blackberries.* New York: Scholastic. Jamie is stung by bees and dies of an allergic reaction. Issues of friendship, playing, and death surface as I use this book with students.

Smith, Robert. (1984). *The War with Grandpa.* New York: Bantam Doubleday. Grandpa needs to live with Peter's family, which means Peter loses his bedroom. Peter tries many mean ways to get his room back.

Speir, Peter. (1980). *People.* Garden City, NY: Doubleday. A classic big book that shows all of the wonderful differences in humans, ending with a representation of how dull the world would be if we were all alike.

Turner, Ann. (1987). *Nettie's Trip South.* New York: Aladdin. In 1859, a young girl goes South with her older brother who is a reporter. She is forever changed when she witnesses a slave auction. A powerful picture book.

Uchida, Yoshiko. (1978). *Journey Home.* Fairfield, PA: Athaneum. I use this either as a read-aloud chapter book or for book groups. It tells the story of a Japanese American family after their release from Topaz, a World War II concentration camp. It is an important story for students to experience.

Whelan, Gloria. (1993). *Goodbye, Vietnam.* New York: Random House. This chapter book helps students internalize some of the experiences of the 60,000 boat people fleeing the Vietnam War to Hong Kong. The families risk their lives, experience hunger and thirst, and then endure the refugee camp. The story brings up the many issues of refugees and immigration.

Williams, Laura. (1996). *Behind the Bedroom Wall.* Minneapolis: Milkweed Editions. This powerful novel, about a 13-year-old girl in a Nazi youth group, elicits deep discussions on many issues—disagreements with parents, mind control, uniforms, meanness, sympathy, hate, values, risking for rightness, enemies, police actions, and more.

Viorst, Judith. (1973). *Alexander and the Terrible, Horrible, No Good, Very Bad Day.* London: Angus & Robertson. A wonderful, picture book story of a young boy having a bad day and realizing "some days are like that."

Vos, Ida. (1986). *Anna Is Still Here*. New York: Scholastic. After three years of hiding, Anna is free and united with her parents. But her spirit is still locked away, her friends are gone, and her fears dominate her recovery.

Vos, Ida. (1981). *Hide and Seek*. New York: Scholastic. As the Nazis invade Holland, Rachel's life becomes restricted. Finally, in hiding, moving from house to house, her family is separated. War is seen through children's eyes.

Wyeth, Sharon Dennis. (1998). *Always My Dad*. New York: Knopf. A picture book about a girl who lives with her grandparents and rarely sees her dad.

Yashima, Taro. (1969). *Crow Boy*. New York: Viking. You can feel the Japanese countryside and a rural schoolhouse where a small boy feels isolated from the other children. Everyone learns in the process of understanding Crow Boy.

Yolen, Jane. (1990). *The Devil's Arithmetic*. New York: Penguin. Hannah often complained about listening to stories about the Holocaust but somehow she opens a door during Passover and finds herself back in Poland in the 1940s.

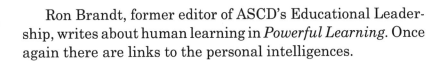

RESOURCE
B

Powerful Learning

Ron Brandt, former editor of ASCD's Educational Leadership, writes about human learning in *Powerful Learning*. Once again there are links to the personal intelligences.

- "People learn what is personally meaningful to them." Meaning is made by the person. We must link to prior knowledge and personally connect new ideas with what we already know, feel, and believe—intrapersonal, internal connections.

- "People learn more when they accept challenging but achievable goals." What is challenging and what is achievable is interpreted by our self-knowledge and self-confidence (intrapersonal connections).

- "Learning is developmental." Particularly important developmental learning is learning to soothe oneself, learning to trust others, and learning to focus one's attention . . . all within intrapersonal intelligence.

- "Individuals learn differently." We have much to learn about our diversity, but understanding our own styles is an important factor in intrapersonal self-management, and understanding others' styles is important for interpersonal effectiveness.

- "Much learning occurs through social interaction." We humans are social. Clearly we learn from interacting

171

with others. However, it is very difficult to be effective socially, interpersonally, if you do not have significant intrapersonal self-management skills.

- "People need feedback to learn." Feedback, whether self-reflection or reflections of other people, is necessary to evaluate your current behavior and make plans for future experiences.

- "Successful learning involves use of strategies—which themselves are learned." Strategies for effective self-management are critical for continual growth. Self-management includes emotional factors, identifying our emotions, soothing ourselves, and deciding on a course of action involving other people. Self-management also includes what we put into our bodies and the exercise routines we adhere to. Reflection strategies, goal setting, and evaluating our progress toward goals are all part of our learned strategies.

- "A positive emotional climate strengthens learning." A positive emotional environment is linked to better quality motivation, enhanced memory, increased attentiveness, and the willingness to take risks in the learning process. It is crucial to positive intrapersonal development and "indispensable to sound education," state Caine and Caine (1997).

- "Learning is influenced by the total environment." Our self-management system scans everything in our environment at all times. The smallest deviation in our environment would be noted and evaluated if it was of concern or not. That means we are physically and emotionally evaluating every stimulation around us, all the time. It means our world of others is continually scanned. Our world of self is also constantly scanned for relevant changes. Our personal world and our interpersonal world connect continually as we experience new learning (Brandt, 1998, pp. 3-12).

HOW STUDENTS LEARN

Published by the American Psychological Association, *How Students Learn* makes powerful statements about how students learn best. Reflect on how many statements relate to the domains of intrapersonal and interpersonal intelligences.

- "Students learn best when they actively construct their own meaning."
- "Students learn best when they use metacognition and self-assessment."
- "Students learn best when they have experience in applying and transferring their knowledge."
- "Students learn best when problems are interesting, meaningful, challenging and engaging."
- "Students learn best when they exercise choice, control, and personal responsibility."
- "Students learn best when they have a sense of efficacy."
- "Students learn best when they work in groups." (Lambert, 1998, pp. 217-220)

The concepts of intrapersonal and interpersonal intelligences came from Howard Gardner's thoughts in the 1980s, but they are linked to many other sources of thoughts in the present. The personal intelligences are rooted in self-management and the ability to work well with others. Their implications are significantly broad.

THE SCHOOLS OUR CHILDREN DESERVE

In his book *The Schools Our Children Deserve*, Alfie Kohn provides a list titled "What To Look For in a Classroom." Included in his list are the following points:

- A room overflowing with books, art supplies, plants, science materials
- Different activities taking place simultaneously
- A gathering place for the whole class
- Teacher's voice respectful, genuine, warm
- Students engaged, eager to explain what they're doing
- Teacher working with small groups or consulting with individuals
- Student projects evident on the walls, in the halls (Kohn, 1999, p. 236-237)

Figure B.1 New Haven Curriculum Scope for Different Age Groups

	Preschool/Early Elementary (K–2) School	Elementary/Intermediate	Middle School	High School
Personal				
Emotion	• Can appropriately express and manage fear, helplessness, anger, affection, excitement, enthusiasm, and disappointment • Can differentiate and label negative and positive emotions in self and others • Increasing tolerance for frustration	• Expressing feelings in positive ways • Controlling own anger • Labeling observed emotions • Harmonizing of others' feelings	• Self-aware and self-critical • Harmonizing of own feelings	All areas should be approached as integrative: • Listening and oral communication • Competence in reading, writing, and computation • Learning to learn skills • Personal management: self-esteem, goal-setting/self-motivation • Personal and moral evaluations of self, actions, behaviors • Beginning to focus on the future • Exploring meaning of one's life, life in general, transcendence • Taking care of self, recognizing consequences of risky behaviors (sexual activity, drug use), protecting self from negative consequences • Harmonizing of own and others' feelings • Adaptability: creative thinking and problem solving, especially in response to barriers/obstacles • Earning and budgeting money • Planning a career and preparing for adult role • Personal career development/goals—pride in work accomplished
Cognition	• Beginning to take a reflective perspective—role taking—what is the other seeing? What is the other feeling? What is the other thinking? What is the other intending? What is the other like? • Generating alternative possibilities for interpersonal actions • Emphasis on attention-sustaining skills, recall and linkage of material, verbalization of coping and problem-solving strategies used	• Knowing about healthy foods and exercising • Times when cooperation, planning are seen; at times, shows knowledge that there is more than one way to solve a problem • Setting goals, anticipating consequences, working to overcome obstacles • Focusing on strengths of self and others • Ability to think through problem situations and anticipate occurrences	• Recognizing the importance of alcohol and other drug abuse and prevention • Establishing norms for health • Setting realistic short-term goals • Seeing both sides of issues, disputes, arguments • Comparing abilities to others, self, or normative standards; abilities considered in light of others' reactions • Acknowledging the importance of self-statements and self-rewards	

174

Figure B1. New Haven Curriculum Scope for Different Age Groups *(continued)*

	Preschool/Early Elementary (K–2) School	Elementary/Intermediate	Middle School	High School
Behavior	• Learning self-management (e.g., when waiting one's turn; when entering and leaving classrooms at the start and end of the day and other transition times; when working on something in a group or alone) • Learning social norms about appearance (e.g., washing face or hair, brushing teeth) • Recognizing dangers to health and safety (e.g., crossing street, electrical sockets, pills that look like candy) • Being physically healthy—adequate nutrition; screenings to identify visual, hearing, language problems	• Understanding safety issues such as interviewing people at the door when home alone; saying no to strangers on the phone or in person • Managing time • Showing respect for others • Can ask for, give, and receive help • Negotiating disputes, deescalating conflicts • Admitting mistakes, apologizing when appropriate	• Initiating own activities • Emerging leadership skills	
Integration	• Integrating feeling and thinking with language, replacing or complementing that which can be expressed only in action, image, or affectivity • Differentiating the emotions, needs, and feelings of different people in different contexts—if not spontaneously, then in response to adult prompting and assistance • Recognizing and resisting inappropriate touching, sexual behaviors	• Ability to calm self down when upset and to verbalize what happened and how one is feeling differently • Encouraging perspective taking and empathic identification with others • Learning strategies for coping with, communicating about, and managing strong feelings	• Being aware of sexual factors, recognizing and accepting body changes, recognizing and resisting inappropriate sexual behaviors • Developing skills for analyzing stressful social situations, identifying feelings, goals, carrying out request and refusal skills	
Key concepts	honesty, fairness, trust, hope, confidence, keeping promises, empathy	initiative, purpose, goals, justice, fairness, friendship, equity, dependability, pride, creativity	democracy, pioneering, importance of the environment (spaceship Earth, earth as habitat, ecological environment, global interdependence, ecosystems), perfection and imperfection, prejudice, freedom, citizenship, liberty, home, industriousness, continuity, competence	relationships, healthy relationships, fidelity, intimacy, love, responsibility, commitment, respect, love and loss, caring, knowledge, growth, human commonalities, work/workplace, emotional intelligence, spirituality, ideas, inventions, identity, self-awareness

175

Figure B1. Curriculum Scope for Different Age Groups (*continued*)

	Preschool/Early Elementary (K–2) School	Elementary/Intermediate	Middle School	High School
Peers/social	• Being a member of a group: sharing, listening, taking turns, cooperating, negotiating disputes, being considerate and helpful • Initiating interactions • Can resolve conflict without fighting; compromising • Understands justifiable self-defense • Empathetic toward peers: showing emotional distress when others are suffering; developing a sense of helping rather than hurting or neglecting; respecting rather than belittling, and supporting and protecting rather than dominating others; awareness of the thoughts, feelings, and experiences of others (perspective taking)	• Listening carefully • Conducting a reciprocal conversation • Using tone of voice, eye contact, posture, and language appropriate to peers (and adults) • Skills for making friends, entering peer groups—can judge peers' feelings, thoughts, plans, actions • Learning to include and exclude others • Expanding peer groups • Friendships based on mutual trust and assistance • Shows altruistic behavior among friends • Becoming assertive, self-calming, cooperative • Learning to cope with peer pressure to conform (e.g., dress) • Learning to set boundaries, to deal with secrets • Dealing positively with rejection	• Choosing friends thoughtfully but aware of group norms, popular trends • Developing peer leadership skills • Dealing with conflict among friends • Recognizing and accepting alternatives to aggression and violence • Belonging is recognized as very important	• Effective behavior in peer groups • Peer leadership/responsible membership • Using request and refusal skills • Initiating and maintaining cross-gender friends and romantic relationships • Understanding responsible behavior at social events • Dealing with drinking and driving

Figure B1. New Haven Curriculum Scope for Different Age Groups *(continued)*

	Preschool/Early Elementary (K–2) School	Elementary/Intermediate	Middle School	High School
Family	• Being a family member: being considerate and helpful, expressing caring, and developing capacity for intimacy • Making contributions at home—chores, responsibilities • Relating to siblings—sharing, taking turns, initiating interactions, negotiating disputes, helping, caring • Internalizing values modeled in family • Self-confident and trusting—what they can expect from adults; believe that they are important; that their needs and wishes matter; that they can succeed; that they can trust their care givers; that adults can be helpful • Intellectually inquisitive—like to explore their home and the world around them • Homes (and communities) free from violence • Home life includes consistent, stimulating contact with caring adults	• Understanding different family forms and structures • Cooperating around household tasks • Acknowledging compliments • Valuing own uniqueness as individual and as family contributor • Sustaining positive interactions with parents and other adult relatives, friends • Showing affection, negative feelings appropriately • Being close, establishing intimacy and boundaries • Accepting failure/difficulty and continuing effort	• Recognizing conflict between parents' and peers' values (e.g., dress, importance of achievement) • Learning about stages in adults' and parents' lives • Valuing of rituals	• Becoming independent • Talking with parents about daily activities, learning self-disclosure skills • Preparing for parenting, family responsibilities

Figure B1. New Haven Curriculum Scope for Different Age Groups *(continued)*

	Preschool/Early Elementary (K–2) School	Elementary/Intermediate	Middle School	High School
School-related				
Reasonable expectations	• Paying attention to teachers • Understanding similarities and differences (e.g., skin color, physical disabilities) • Working to the best of one's ability • Using words effectively, especially for feelings • Cooperating • Responding positively to approval • Thinking out loud, asking questions • Expressing self in art, music games, dramatic play • Likes starting more than finishing • Deriving security in repetition, routines • Able to articulate likes and dislikes, has clear sense of strengths, areas of mastery, can articulate these, and has opportunities to engage in these • Exploring the environment • Self-confident and trusting—what they can expect from adults in the school; believing that they are important; that their needs and wishes matter; that they can succeed; that they can trust adults in school; that adults in school can be helpful	• Setting academic goals, planning study time, completing assignments • Learning to work on teams • Accepting similarities and differences (e.g., appearance, ability levels) • Cooperating, helping—especially helping younger children • Bouncing back from mistakes • Able to work hard on projects • Beginning, carrying through on, and completing tasks • Good problem solving • Forgiving after anger • Generally truthful • Showing pride in accomplishments • Can calm down after being upset, losing one's temper, or crying • Able to follow directions for school tasks, routines • Carrying out commitments to classmates, teachers • Showing appropriate helpfulness • Knowing how to ask for help • Refusing negative peer pressure	• Will best accept modified rules • Enjoys novelty over repetition • Can learn planning and management skills to complete school requirements	• Making a realistic academic plan, recognizing personal strengths, persisting to achieve goals in spite of setbacks • Planning a career/post-high school pathways • Group effectiveness: interpersonal skills, negotiation, teamwork • Organizational effectiveness and leadership—making a contribution to classroom and school

Figure B1. New Haven Curriculum Scope for Different Age Groups *(continued)*

	Preschool/Early Elementary (K–2) School	Elementary/Intermediate	Middle School	High School
Appropriate Environment	• Clear classroom, school rules • Opportunities for responsibility in the classroom • Authority clear, fair, deserving of respect • Frequent teacher redirection • Classrooms and school-related locations free from violence and threat • School life includes consistent, stimulating contact with caring adults	• Opportunities to comfort peer or classmate in distress, help new persons feel accepted/included • Being in groups, group activities • Making/using effective group rules • Participating in story-based learning • Opportunities to negotiate • Time for laughter, occasional silliness	• Minimizing lecture-mode of instruction • Varying types of student products (deemphasize written reports) • Opportunities to participate in setting policy • Clear expectations about truancy, substance use, violent behavior • Opportunities for setting, reviewing personal norms/standards • Group/academic/extracurricular memberships	• Guidance/structures for goal setting, future planning, post-school transition • Opportunities for participating in school service and other nonacademic involvement • Being a role model for younger students
Community	• Curiosity about how and why things happen • Recognizing a pluralistic society (e.g., aware of holidays, customs, cultural groups) • Accepting responsibility for the environment • Participating in community events (e.g., religious observances, recycling)	• Joining groups outside the school • Learning about, accepting cultural, community differences • Helping people in need	• Understanding and accepting differences in one's community • Identifying and resisting negative group influences • Developing involvements in community projects • Apprenticing/training for leadership roles	• Contributing to community service or environmental projects • Accepting responsibility for the environment • Understanding elements of employment • Understanding issues of government
Events Triggering Preventive Services	• Coping with divorce • Dealing with death in the family • Becoming a big brother or big sister • Dealing with family moves	• Coping with divorce • Dealing with death in the family • Becoming a big brother or big sister • Dealing with family moves	• Coping with divorce • Dealing with death in the family • Dealing with a classmate's drug use or delinquent behavior	• Coping with divorce • Dealing with death in the family • Dealing with a classmate's drug use or delinquent behavior, injury or death due to violence, pregnancy, suicide, HIV/AIDS • Transition from high school to workplace, college, living away from home

SOURCE: From *Promoting Social and Emotional Learning Guidelines for Educators.* By Maurice J. Elias, Joseph E. Zins, Roger P. Weissberg, Karin S. Frey, Mark T. Greenburg, Norris M. Haynes, Rachael Kessler, Mary E. Schwab-Stone, and Timothy P. Shriver. Alexandria, VA: Association for Supervision and Curriculum Development. Copyright @ 1997 ACSD. Reprinted by permission. All rights reserved.

Figure B.2 Week in Review

THE WEEK IN REVIEW

Today's date: _____

Your name (if you want to give it): _____

Think back on the past week in this classroom. Read each statement, then check the column that best describes how you feel about your week.

This week in school:	All of the time	Most of the time	Some of the time	Never
1. I was respected as a person.				
2. I treated others with respect.				
3. I was treated fairly.				
4. I treated others fairly.				
5. People helped me when I needed help.				
6. I helped others.				
7. We cared for each other.				
8. We worked hard to make our classroom a positive place to be.				
9. I felt like I belonged.				
10. I helped others feel like they belonged.				
11. I was encouraged to do my best.				
12. I encouraged others to do their best.				
13. We worked together to solve problems.				
14. We cooperated with each other.				
15. I felt accepted.				
16. I helped others feel accepted.				

RESOURCE
C

A List of Emotional Vocabulary

absorbed	adventurous	affectionate	alert	alive
amazed	amused	aggressive	alienated	angry
animated	abandoned	attacked	apathetic	abused
appreciative	astonished	aroused	aggravated	antsy
anxious	astounded	anguished	agitated	alarmed
ashamed	annoyed	apathetic	aloof	afraid
ambitious	analytical	assertive	aware	attentive
bashful	bewildered	betrayed	bullied	blissful
breathless	buoyant	brokenhearted	blah	bored
cautious	confident	confused	curious	cross
cheerful	cheated	concerned	chagrined	cruel
courageous	conscientious	cooperative	courteous	calm
disappointed	disturbed	depressed	down	dazzled
determined	discouraged	disgusted	droopy	dull
despondent	disenchanted	disgruntled	dismayed	delighted
diminished	distrusted	distressed		
embarrassed	enthusiastic	envious	energetic	excited
exhausted	exasperated	embittered	ecstatic	eager
empathetic	efficient			

fascinated	friendly	free	fidgety	foolish
fulfilled	fatigued	frightened	frustrated	fearful
forgotten	furious	forlorn		
gloomy	guilty	glorious	great	good
grouchy	grumpy	good-humored	glowing	glad
grateful	gratified	gleeful		
happy	hopeless	helpless	horrible	hurt
hateful	homesick	hostile	harried	hot
horrified	hesitant	heavy	helpful	
interrupted	intimidated	inquisitive	inspired	intense
impatient	indifferent	intrigued	irritated	irate
inspiring	interested	involved	irked	industrious
imaginative	ingenious	independent		
jealous	joyful	jumpy	jittery	jubilant
kind	keyed-up	knocked-down	kindly	keen
lonesome	lethargic	listless	loving	low
left out	let down	leery	lazy	lost
likable	lively	loyal		
miserable	mixed-up	mournful	morose	mean
mellow	mirthful	melodramatic	merry	moved
manipulated	misunderstood	meddlesome	mopey	mad
naughty	nervous	nettled	numb	nice
optimistic	overwhelmed	oppositional	overjoyed	ordained
panicked	petrified	picked-on	playful	positive
pessimistic	perplexed	pleased	proud	polite
peaceful	pathetic	puzzled	pretty	pleasant
patronized	pressured	provoked	put-down	passive
refreshed	rejected	relieved	relaxed	rested
radiant	rancorous	reluctant	resentful	restless

resourceful	responsible	resilient	reliable	

sorrowful	skeptical	sad	stable	spirited
satisfied	spellbound	sensitive	splendid	secure
stimulated	surprised	spiritless	startled	sorry
suspicious	shocked	silly	scared	self-assured
successful	strong			

troubled	terrified	terrible	tense	tired
thankful	tranquil	trusting	tender	tepid
trustworthy	tenderhearted	thoughtful	tolerant	tactful

uncomfortable	unconcerned	unnerved	unsteady	upset
unglued	uptight	uncertain	unhappy	uneasy

vexed	violent	valiant	vacant	vague

weary	worried	wide awake	woeful	wistful
withdrawn	wonderful	wretched	wise	witty

yucky

zestful

References

Amen, D. (1998). *Change your brain, change your life.* New York: Random House.

Ashton-Warner, S. (1963). *Teacher.* New York: Simon & Schuster.

Beane, A. (1999). *The bully free classroom.* Minneapolis, MN: Free Spirit Publishing.

Boyer, E. (1983). *High school.* The Carnegie Foundation for the Advancement of Teaching. New York: Harper & Row.

Brandt, R. (1998). *Powerful learning.* Alexandria, VA: Association for Supervision and Curriculum Development.

Brendtro, L., Brokenleg, M., & Van Bockern, S. (1990). *Reclaiming youth at risk.* Bloomington, IN: National Educational Service.

Caine, R. N., & Caine, G. (1991). *Making connections: Teaching and the human brain.* Alexandria, VA: Association for Supervision and Curriculum Development.

Childre, D. L. (1995). *A parenting manual.* Boulder Creek, CA: Planetary Publications.

Childre, D. L. (1996). *Teaching children to love.* Boulder Creek, CA: Planetary Publications.

Cohen, J. (1999). *Educating minds and hearts.* New York: Teachers College Press.

Covey, S. (1991). *Principle-centered leadership.* New York: Simon & Schuster.

Covey, S. (1992). *Principle-centered leadership* (Fireside edition). New York: Simon & Schuster.

Dalton, J., & Watson, M. (1997). *Among friends*. Oakland, CA: Developmental Studies Center.

Damasio, A. (1994). *Descartes' error: Emotion, reason, and the human brain*. New York: Avon.

Damasio, A. (1999). *The feeling of what happens*. New York: Harcourt Brace.

D'Arcangelo, M. (1998, November). The brains behind the brain. *Educational Leadership, 56*(3), 25.

Dewey, J. (1990). *The school and society: The child and the curriculum*. Chicago: University of Chicago Press.

Diamond, M. (1998, November). The brains behind the brain. *Educational Leadership, 56*(3).

Diamond, M., & Hopson, J. (1998). *Magic trees of the mind*. New York: Penguin.

Dresser, N. (1994). *I felt like I was from another planet*. Menlo Park, CA: Addison-Wesley.

Dryer, S. S. (1993). *The bookfinder* (Vol. 5). Circle Pines, MN: American Guidance Service.

Elias, M., Zins, J., Weissberg, R., Frey, K., Greenberg, M., Haynes, N., Kessler, R., Schwab-Stone, M., & Shriver, T. (1997). *Promoting social and emotional learning: Guidelines for educators*. Alexandria, VA: Association for Supervision and Curriculum Development.

Ellison, L. (1993). *Seeing with magic glasses*. Atlanta, GA: Great Ocean.

Espeland, P., & Wallner, R. (1991). *Making the most of today*. Minneapolis, MN: Free Spirit Publishing.

Fauber, J. (1999, May 12). Abuse can rewire kids' brains, study says. *Milwaukee Journal Sentinel*, p. 1.

Fisher, C. W., & Berliner, D. C. (Eds.). (1995). *Perspectives on instructional time*. White Plains, NY: Longman.

Fiske, E. (1991). *Smart schools, smart kids*. New York: Simon & Schuster.

Gardner, H. (1983). *Frames of mind: The theory of multiple intelligences*. New York: Basic Books.

Gardner, H. (1993). *Multiple intelligences: The theory in practice*. New York: Basic Books.

Gardner, H. (1997). *Extraordinary minds*. New York: Basic Books.

Gardner, H. (1999a). *The disciplined mind: What all students should understand*. New York: Simon & Schuster.

Gardner, H. (1999b). *Intelligence reframed: Multiple intelligences for the 21st century*. New York: Basic Books.

Given, B. (1998, November). Food for thought. *Educational Leadership*, 68-71.

Goleman, D. (1997, May). Up with emotional health. *Educational Leadership, 54*(8), 12-14.

Goleman, D. (1998). *Emotional intelligence.* New York: Bantam.

Grade level expectations. (1998). Minneapolis, MN Public Schools.

Greenberg, M., & Snell, J. (1997). Brain development and emotional development: The role of teaching in organizing the frontal lobe. In P. Salovey, & D. J. Sluyter (Eds.), *Emotional development and emotional intelligence.* New York: Basic Books.

Greenspan, S. (1993). *Playground politics: Understanding the emotional life of your school-age child.* Reading, MA: Perseus.

Greenspan, S. (1997). *The growth of the mind.* Reading, MA: Addison-Wesley.

Hargreaves, A. (Ed.). (1997). *Rethinking educational change with heart and mind.* Alexandria, VA: Association for Supervision and Curriculum Development.

Healy, J. (1998). *Failure to connect.* New York: Simon & Schuster.

Hendrix, H., & Hunt, H. (1997). *Giving the love that heals.* New York: Simon & Schuster.

Holbrook, M. L. (1884). *Hygiene of the brain.* New York: John W. Lovell.

Humphrey, J. H. (1988). *Teaching children to relax.* Springfield, IL: Charles C Thomas.

James, B. (1994). *Handbook for treatment of attachment-trauma problems in children.* New York: Lexington Books.

Jensen, E. (1998). *Teaching with the brain in mind.* Alexandria, VA: Association for Supervision and Curriculum Development.

Justice, B. (1987). *Who gets sick: Thinking and health.* Houston, TX: Peak Press.

Karr-Morse, R., & Wiley, M. (1997). *Ghosts from the nursery.* New York: Atlantic Monthly.

Keirsey, D., & Bates, M. (1978). *Please understand me.* Del Mar, CA: Prometheus Nemesis.

Kincher, J. (1990). *Psychology for kids.* Minneapolis, MN: Free Spirit Publishing.

King, M. (1988, Winter). Ordinary Olympians. *In Context, 18,* 14-15.

Kohn, A. (1993). *Punished by rewards.* New York: Houghton Mifflin.

Kohn, A. (1999). *The schools our children deserve.* New York: Houghton Mifflin.

Kotulak, R. (1996). *Inside the brain: Revolutionary discoveries of how the mind works.* Kansas City, MO: Universal Press.

Kriete, R. (1999). *The morning meeting book.* Greenfield, MA: Northeast Foundation for Children.

Lambert, N. M., & McCombs, B. L. (1998). *How students learn: Reforming schools through learner-centered education.* Washington, DC: American Psychological Association.

Langer, E. (1997). *The power of mindful learning.* Reading, MA: Addison-Wesley.

LeDoux, J. (1996). *The emotional brain.* New York: Simon & Schuster.

Levine, B. H. (1991). *Your body believes every word you say.* Boulder Creek, CA: Aslan.

Lewis, C. (1995). *Educating hearts and minds.* Cambridge, UK: Cambridge University Press.

Lewis, C., & Tsuchida, I. (1998, March). The basics in Japan: The three C's. *Educational Leadership,* 32-37.

Lowenthal, B. (1999, Summer). Effects of maltreatment and ways to promote children's resiliency. *Childhood Education,* 205.

Mandela, N. (1994). *Long walk to freedom.* London: Little, Brown.

Marx, E., & Wooley, S. F. (Eds.). (1998). *Health is academic.* New York: Teachers College Press.

McIntosh, P., & Style, E. (1999). Social, emotional, and political learning. In J. Cohen (Ed.), *Educating minds and hearts.* New York: Teachers College Press.

Meichenbaum, D., & Biemiller, A. (1998). *Nurturing independent learners: Helping students take charge of their learning.* Cambridge, MA: Brookline.

New City School. (1996). *Succeeding with multiple intelligences: Teaching through the personal intelligences.* St. Louis, MO: Author.

National Middle Schools Association. (1998, September). *A platform for effective middle grades education in the Minneapolis (MN) public schools.* Minneapolis, MN: Author.

Palmer, P. (1998). *The courage to teach.* San Francisco: Jossey-Bass.

Payne, R. (1995). *A framework for understanding and working with students and adults from poverty.* Baytown, TX: RFT Publishing.

Pert, C. (1997). *Molecules of emotion.* New York: Scribner.

Sacks, O. (1986). *The man who mistook his wife for a hat.* London: Duckworth.

Salovey, P., & Sluyter, D. J. (Eds.). (1997). *Emotional development and emotional intelligence: Educational implications.* New York: Basic Books.

Sapolsky, R. (1994). *Why zebras don't get ulcers.* New York: Freeman.

Shriver, T. P. (with Schwab-Stone, M., & DeFalco, K.). (1999). Why SEL is the better way. In J. Cohen (Ed.), *Educating minds and hearts*. New York: Teachers College Press.

Smith, P. (1980). *Total breathing*. New York: McGraw-Hill.

Spier, P. (1980). *People*. New York: Doubleday.

Sylwester, R. (1997a). *A celebration of neurons: An educator's guide to the human brain*. Alexandria, VA: Association for Supervision and Curriculum Development.

Sylwester, R. (1997b). *Electronic media and brain development* [video]. Tuscon, AZ: Zephyr.

Sylwester, R. (1998, November). Art for the brain's sake. *Educational Leadership,* 31-35.

Sylwester, R. (2000). *A biological brain in a cultural classroom*. Thousand Oaks, CA: Corwin.

Tanner, L. (1997). *Dewey's laboratory school: Lessons for today*. New York: Teachers College Press.

Tieger, P. D., & Barron-Tieger, B. (1997). *Nurture by nature*. Boston: Little, Brown.

Tomlinson, C. A. (1999). *The differentiated classroom*. Alexandria, VA: Association for Supervision and Curriculum Development.

Wasserman, S. (1989, Summer). Children working in groups? It doesn't work! *Childhood Education,* 201-205.

Wellness Reproductions and Publishing. (n.d.). *Emotions vocabulary FLASHCARDS*. Beachwood, OH: Author.

Wheatley, M., & Kellner-Rogers, M. (1996). *A simpler way*. San Francisco: Berrett-Koehler.

Whetzel, D. (1992, March). *ERIC clearinghouse on tests, measurement, and evaluation*. Washington, DC. Retrieved February 17, 2000, from the World Wide Web: http:www.ed.gov/databases/ERIC_Digests/ed339749.html

Witkin, G. (1999). *KidStress*. New York: Penguin.

Wolfe, P., & Brandt, R. (1998, November). What do we know from brain research? *Educational Leadership,* 8-13.

Wood, C. (1999). *Time to teach, time to learn*. Greenfield, MA: Northeast Foundation for Children.

Wood, G. (1992). *Schools that work*. New York: Penguin.

Index

Absenteeism, 105-107
Abstract thought, 49. *See also* Thinking
Abused children, 102-103
Activity, physical, 19-20
ADD (Attention Deficit Disorder), 95-97, 116-117, 159
ADHD (Attention Deficit Hyperactivity Disorder), 95-97, 116-117
Adopted children, 112
Aggressive behavior, 54-56, 100-103. *See also* Attention and behavior
Amygdala, 48, 53, 56
Anger, 51, 100-103. *See also* Attention and behavior
Art programs, school:
   Responsive Classroom and, 147-148
   symbolic messages and, 70
Ashton-Warner, Sylvia, 13
Assessments, designing, 130, 137
Assignments:
   monitoring for success, 59-61
   responsibility of, 82-83
   studying famous people, 66-70
Association for Supervision and Curriculum Development (ASCD), 150-151
Attention and behavior:
   chemical influences on, 54-55, 101-102
   directing (focusing), 4, 46-50, 85-86, 91-92, 114-116, 159-160

Attention Deficit Disorder (ADD), children with, 95-97, 116-117, 159
Attention-sorting process, 4, 46-50. *See also* Attention and behavior
Attitudes, internal, 80-81, 104-105. *See also* Emotions
Auditory learners, 48, 110, 119-120

Babies. *See* Infants
Basal ganglia function, 96, 117
Beginning of school. *See* First days of school
Behavior. *See* Attention and behavior
Behavior domains, 10
Body messages, 80-81, 114. *See also* Brain (mind); Stress
Body systems, teaching about, 65-66
Body tension, 97-98. *See also* Stress
Book list, 163-170. *See also* Teacher resources
Bookfinder, The, 163
Brain (mind):
   and the body, 23, 42-45
   attention-sorting process, 4, 46-48, 115-116
   levels of processing, 3-5
   nutritional issues, 25-26, 36, 63-65
   See also Emotions
Brain stem, 3-4
Brainstorming, 66
Brandt, Ron, 171

Breakfasts, healthy, 26, 64
Breathing tips, 24, 25
Bulletin boards, 8
Bully Free Classroom, The, 156, 180
BullyProof, 155

Calming skills, 21, 22-25, 97-98. *See also*
    Stress
Cause and effect, understanding, 82-83, 160
Children:
    adopted, 112
    bright and emotionally sensitive, 98-99
    bright and insecure, 97-98
    differences in, 61-62, 94-95
    emotional development of, 16, 46-50
    40 developmental assets for, 139-141
    "I'm not doing nothing," 104-105
    in crisis, 100-103
    refugee, 103-104
    unfocused, 105-107
    with ADHD, 95-97, 116-117
    with learned helplessness, 26, 99-100,
        132
Child's play, 19-20
Choices, student, 26-27, 132-133
Class meetings, 59
Classroom environment:
    creating community focused, 1-3
    physical arrangement, 2-3, 4, 173
    See also Symbolic messages
Coles, Robert, 70
Collaboration, process of learning, 90, 133,
    161
Collaborative for the Advancement of Social
    and Emotional Learning (CASEL), 150
Commitment, teacher, 17, 108-109, 143
Conferences, teacher, 79-80, 84, 86
Conflict resolution, 28-35, 40, 136
Consequences, 61
Content, integration of, 130-133
Cooperative groups, 90, 131-133, 161
Criminal behavior, 34. *See also* Attention
    and behavior
Cross-age tutoring, 62-63
Cultural differences, understanding, 108,
    134
Curriculum experience:
    choices teachers make, 44, 57, 108-109,
        113
    Friendly Helpers, 62-63
    functional and symbolic messages within,
        57-58, 161

human body study, 65-66
    monitoring for success, 11, 59-62
    poor nutrition, effects of, 63-65
    research skills, teaching, 66-70
    two-hour work blocks, 58-59
Curriculum standards, 141-142

Damasio, Antonio, 29, 44
Darwin, Charles, 51
Decision making skills, 47, 117
Descartes, René, 43
Descartes' Error (Damasio), 44
Dewey, John, 11
Diversity:
    awareness of our, 94-95, 117-124, 160
    concept of, 61-62, 67, 108-109
    graphing (math lesson), 111-113
    in brain development, child, 116-117
    in perceptual strengths, 14, 109-110
    in self-awareness, 114-116
    in self-management skills, 113-114
    Introvert/Extrovert preferences, 110-
        111
Dopamine, high levels of, 64, 117
Dresser, Norine, 153
Dunn, Rita and Ken, 122

Education, implications of neurobiology for,
    145-146
Emotion puppets, 30-32, 136-137
Emotional hijacking, 21, 36, 53, 100
Emotional intelligence, 42-43
Emotional Intelligence (Goleman), 43, 159
Emotional processing, 5, 21, 41, 43, 53-56
Emotional vocabulary:
    list of, 181-183
    teaching, 27-28, 136-137, 148
Emotions:
    and learning, affects of, 41-42
    and personal intelligence, 42-45
    as organizing force, 45-46
    chemistry of, 50-53
    connecting their, 66-70
    developmental issues, 16, 46-50, 101,
        117, 133-134
    processing, 5, 21, 41, 43, 53-56
    See also Attention and behavior;
        Reflective activities; Stress
Empathy, teaching, 49, 68, 72, 133-137,
    153, 161
Environmental factors, 122
ESL students, 103-104

Exercise. *See* Child's play; Food habits
Exhaustion, nervous, 14
Expectations, overarching goals, 138-139
Extrinsic motivation, 130-131
Extroverted preferences, 110-111, 118-119

Failure to Connect (Healy), 91
Fear response, 48, 56, 100
Feelings, 29, 50
Fight or flight response, 100. *See also*
    Emotional processing
Finger agnosia, 96
First days of school, goals for, 5-9
Focused attention. *See* Attention and
    behavior
Food habits:
    and brain function, 63-65
    and stress, 25-26
40 Developmental Assets for Elementary-
    Age Children, 139-141
Frames of Mind (Gardner), 9, 15, 42
Freeze Frame, 35-39
Friendly Helpers, 62-63
Friendship building, 8
Frontal lobes, 47, 55-56, 115, 117

Gardner, Howard, concept of multiple
    intelligence, 9-10, 15, 42, 123, 158
Generational poverty, 127
Goal setting, reflective:
    exploring ideas, 8-9
    having a clear image, 81-82
    three-way process, 79-81
Goleman, Daniel, 21, 36, 43, 113, 159
Gratification, delayed, 113-114, 149
Greenspan, Stanley, 44
Growth of the Mind, The (Greenspan), 44
Guided discovery, 150

Handwriting, 96
Health education, 63-65
Healy, Jane, 91
Helpers, friendly, 62-63
Helplessness, sense of, 26, 99-100, 132
High-risk behaviors, 151-152. *See also*
    Attention and behavior
Homeostasis (balance), 4
Homework, 60, 82-83

How Students Learn, 172-173
Hubel, David, 3

I Felt Like I Was From Another Planet
    (Dresser), 153
"I" statements, 28-30
Immune system, 18-19
Impulse control, 113-114
Impulsive behavior, 54-55, 100-103. *See*
    also ADHD
Independent learners, nurturing:
    content choice, 132
    cooperative groups, 133
    extrinsic motivation, 130-131
    importance of, 125-130
    sample rubric, 129, 130
    self-instruction, examples of, 128
Individual differences, 61-62, 94-95. *See*
    also Children; Diversity
Infants, emotional development of, 34, 46-
    50, 133-333
Information processing, 85-86
Inner speech, modeling. *See* self-talk
Inner voice, 91
Insecurity, feelings of, 97-98
Institute of HeartMath, 35, 37
Intelligence:
    emotional, 42-43
·   multiple view of, 9-10, 15, 42, 66-70, 123,
    158
Intelligence Reframed (Gardner), 10
Intention. *See* Attention and behavior
Interactions, purposeful, 49
Interpersonal intelligence:
    Gardner's definition of, 10-11, 15, 42
    overview of, 158-162
    See also Teacher resources
Intimacy, 48
Intrapersonal intelligence:
    Gardner's definition of, 10-11, 15, 42
    overview of, 158-162
    See also Teacher resources
Introverted preferences, 110-111, 118-119
Intuitive students, 120-121

Japanese elementary schools, central
    qualities of, 131
Journal reflections, 76
Joy, 51
Judgers, 121

Kinesthetic learners, 83, 109-110, 119

Langer, Ellen, 115
Language development, 91, 103

Learned helplessness, 26, 99-100, 132
Learner-centered practices, 137
Learning:
    concepts of, 16, 171-173
    emotions, affects of, 41-45
    See also Stress; Teaching and learning
    goals
Learning styles:
    eight multiple intelligences, 123-124
    environmental factors, 122
    extraverts/introverts, 118-119
    judging and perceiving preferences, 121-
    122
    physical aspects of, 122-123
    sensing and intuition preferences, 119-
    121
    sociological preferences, 122
    thinking and feeling preferences, 121
    understanding, 14, 117-118
    See also Teaching and learning goals
LeDoux, Joseph, 21, 53
Limbic system, 4
Literature, 70-72
Longitudinal portfolio, 92-93
Love, sense of, 48

MacLean, Paul, 3, 4
Maltreatment, emotional, 100
Marshmallow Test, 113
Math lesson (graphing diversity), 111-113
Memories, 5, 23, 45, 47, 56
Midbrain, 4-5, 50
Mind. See Brain (mind)
Mindfulness, 114-116
Mistakes, students', 60
Molecules of Emotion (Pert), 52-53
Montessori, Maria, 14
Morning meetings, 58, 74, 135, 148
Motivation and achievement, 130-131
Multi-age classroom, 61-62
Multiple intelligence:
    definition of, 123-124
    emotional intelligence, 42-43
    Frames of Mind, (Gardner), 9, 15, 42
    Gardner, Howard, concept of multiple
    intelligence, 9-10, 15, 42, 123, 158
    Suceeding With Multiple Intelligences,
    146-147
    See also Intelligence, multiple view of;
    Interpersonal intelligence;
    Intrapersonal intelligence; Kinesthetic

learners; Learning styles; Personal
    intelligences
Murphy-Meisgeiger Type Indicator of
    Children (MMTIC), 118
Muscle relaxation tips, 24
Myers-Briggs Type Indicator (MBTI)
    preferences, 118-121

Nervous system, sympathetic, 18-19
Neurodevelopmental lag, 117
New Haven Schools:
    scope for different age groups, 174-179
    social development curriculum (K-12),
    151-152, 154-155
No-Name Papers, 60
Nonverbals, understanding, 32-35, 49, 159
Noradrenaline, 55, 101-102
Nurturing, early, 48, 133-134
Nutritional issues, 25-26, 63-65

Occipital lobe, 47
Organizational structures, 57-58

Parietal lobe, 47
Paying attention. See Attention and
    behavior
Peer feedback, 84-86
Peptides, 50
Perceivers, 121-122
Perceptual modalities:
    diversity of, 109-110
    understanding preferences, 14, 118-122,
    160
Personal intelligences:
    and emotions, 42-45
    books connecting to, 163-170
    development of, 10-11, 107
    Gardner's concept of, 15
    teaching for, 57-58, 138-139
    See also Teacher resources
Pert, Candace, 50-53
Phonics, 120
"Platform for Effective Middle Grades
    Education," 143
Play, child's, 19-20
Portfolio reflections:
    final presentation, 92-93
    sorting and organizing, concept of, 60, 86-
    89
    See also Reflective activities
Poverty, children of, 94, 105-107, 127

Power of Mindful Learning, The (Langer), 115

Powerful Learning (Brandt), 171-172

Prefrontal cortex, 23, 117

Presentations, modeling, 67

Prior knowledge, 125

Problem-solving skills, 22-25, 30. *See also* Conflict resolution

Promoting Social and Emotional Learning: Guidelines for Educators, 150-151

Proteins, 26, 64-65

Puppets, emotion, 30-32, 136-137

Questioning skills, 27, 78

Racial diversity, 108

Rageful behavior, 100-103. *See also* Attention and behavior

Reactions, automatic, 21, 46, 53. *See also* Emotional processing

Reason and logic, 43, 147

Record system, open, 59-62

Recticular Activating System (RAS), 4

Reflection:
    and internal self-talk, 89-92
    and peer feedback, 84-86
    building skills of, 49-50, 75-76, 82-83, 86
    implications of, 73-75, 93
    See also Portfolio reflections

Reflective activities:
    end of the day reflection, 78-79
    journal reflections, 76
    "Knowing When You Know," 76-78
    portfolios, 86-89, 92-93
    self-evaluations, 75-76
    three-draft scary story, 83-86

Reflective response system, 55-56, 117

Reflective teachers, 6, 73-75

Reflexive response system, 21, 53-56

Refugees, 103-104

Relationships, 11

Relaxation methods, 4, 24

Research skills, teaching, 66-70

Resolving Conflict Creatively Program, 152

Resources. *See* Teacher resources

Responsibility:
    internalization of, 82-83
    shared, 137

Responsive Classroom approach, 147-150

Rhythm, daily, 7, 27

Room design. *See* Classroom environment

Routines, 7, 27

Rubrics, 129, 130

Ruby Bridges (Coles), 70-73

Sacks, Oliver, 34

Sapolsky, Robert, 18

SAT tests, 114

Schools Our Children Deserve, The (Kohn), 173

Second Step, 150

Selective attention, 116

Self-awareness, building, 77-78, 82, 114. *See also* Mindfulness; Reflective activities

Self-care, habits of, 63-65

Self-evaluation, tools of, 75-76, 82, 143. *See also* Reflective activities

Self-instruction, examples of, 128. *See also* Independent learners

Self-knowledge, 7

Self-management, emotional, 82, 98, 113-114, 139

Self-monitoring skills, 59, 117

Self-reflection, habits of, 73-75. *See also* Reflective activities

Self-regulating learners, 130

Self-talk, internal, 83, 89-92, 160

Sensitive students, emotionally, 98-99

Sensor students, 119-120

Sensory experiences, organizing, 4, 44-45, 46-48, 51

Serotonin, low levels of, 26, 54-55, 101-102

Sharing time, student, 149-150

Situational poverty, 127

Social-emotional learning (SEL), 150

Socialization, 49, 117, 148, 150. *See also* Emotions

Sociological factors, of learning styles, 122

Speech, inner:
    prefrontal cortex and, 117
    See also Self-talk

Sperry, Roger, 14

Standards, curriculum, 141-142

Starting Small, 153

Stimuli, distinguishing, 92, 115

Stress:
    chemistry of, 18-19
    child's play and, 19-20
    food and, 25-26
    Freeze Frame process, 35-39
    identifying, 20-21
    managing, 22-25, 97-98
    relaxation methods for, 4, 24, 25

Student teachers, 73-74
Study strategies, effective, 109
Succeeding With Multiple Intelligences,
    146-147
Support, 27
Survival, emotions and, 51
Sylwester, Robert, 21, 53
Symbolic messages:
    idea of functional and, 57-58, 161
    within historical events, 66-70
    within literature, 70-73
    within school arts, 70
Synesthesia, 47

Talk time, 12
Teacher (Ashton-Warner), 13
Teacher resources:
    additional materials, 153, 155-156
    ASCD and CASEL, 150-151
    book list, 163-170
    New Haven's curriculum, 151-152, 154-
        155, 174-179
    Responsive Classroom approach, 147-150
    Second Step, 150
    Succeeding With Multiple Intelligences,
        146-147
    See also Teaching and learning goals
Teacher-center model, 137
Teachers:
    a "reflective-teacher," 6, 73
    commitment of, 17, 108-109, 143
    role of, 44
Teaching and learning goals:
    curriculum standards, 141-142
    developing assets, 139-141
    foundational skills, 143-145
    overarching goals, 138-139
    platform for middle grades, 143

Teaching practices:
    direct skill-based focus, 57
    guides in developing good, 9-17
    learner-centered focus, 137
    reflection and, 6, 75
Teaching Tolerance magazine, 153
TEAM cards, 90
Temporal lobe, 47
Thinkers, 121
Thinking, 46, 49, 53-56
Thought process, 19, 49, 127. *See also*
    Reflection
Three-draft story, 83
Touch sensitive, 48
Triune Brain, 3
Tutoring, cross-age, 62-63

Venn diagram, 71
Violent behavior, 34. *See also* Impulsive
    behavior
Visual learners, 83, 110, 118, 120
Vocabulary, emotional:
    list of, 181-183
    teaching, 27-28, 134-137, 148
Vygotsky, L. S., 26

Water consumption, importance of, 65
Whole-brain education, 14
Why Zebras Don't Get Ulcers (Sapolsky), 18
Willful behavior, 48
Work, saving student's, 86
Work blocks, two-hour, 58-59
Work folders, benefits of, 59-60
Workplace skills, 143-145
Writing skills, 83-86
Written reflection, 76

Zone of proximal development, 126